A Paperback Original
First published 1989 by
Poolbeg Press Ltd.
Knocksedan House,
Swords, Co. Dublin, Ireland.

© Sean McCann 1989

ISBN 1 85371 029 6

Cover design and illustrations by Steven Hope
Cover illustration courtesy of Mr Fothergill's Seeds
Typeset by Print-Forme,
62 Santry Close, Dublin 9.
Printed by The Guernsey Press Ltd.,
Vale, Guernsey, Channel Islands.

GROWING THINGS

SEÁN McCANN

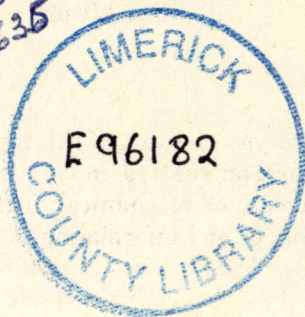

Children's
POOLBEG

The cover illustration is of *Cornfield Mixture* from **Mr Fothergill's Seeds** Wild Flower range. The author and publisher gratefully acknowledge the help of Mr Fothergill's Seeds, Kentford, Suffolk.

Contents

Introduction

here are nearly 400,000 kinds of plants in the world ... some of them so tiny that they can only be seen under a microscope, others are hundreds of feet tall while there are still others that are hard to distinguish from animals.

No one could ever grow them all—but it is amazing just how many plants can be grown in the smallest area and even without a garden. Soil is, of course, the medium that you need to grow most plants successfully but there are some plants that will grow in a glass of water, others in a tiny pot on the window sill; others that only need air to grow, and others need moss around their roots to grow. The plant world is a truly amazing one.

Plants are there for so many reasons—to eat,

to decorate and bring colour to the home, to smell and often, just for fun. Have you ever seen anyone lift a rose without immediately sniffing it? Or seen someone peel an onion without tears streaming from their eyes? That shows you the huge world that exists in just the fragrance of plants.

There is a wonderful sense of excitement when you see the first little plant emerge from the seed that you have sown or a plant that grows tall and strong from what was simply a tiny snip with a couple of leaves and little else. In fact you can reach the stage where you will never throw away a pip from an orange, an apple or the top of a pineapple.

Even the seeds from a Kiwi fruit can be dried and grown on to make a lovely house plant that you can use for your own enjoyment or as a gift for a friend. And did you know that you can plant a number of seeds on a damp piece of cloth or blotting paper, leave it on the windowsill, and in a very short time you could be cutting the results for your sandwiches?

That is what this book is all about. I want to show you just how easy it is to grow plants from the fruits that we eat; how a small conker can eventually grow into a huge chesnut tree; and how to plan your garden or your window sill to the best advantage.

The wonderful thing is that when you begin growing things you set out on a voyage of discovery that will bring excitement, beauty and pleasure into your life—as well as into the lives of many other people.

You never can tell where a small package of annual seeds will lead you. That is the thrill of it all. You don't have to be an expert to grow things. You don't have to know those big Latin and Greek names that the people in horticulture give to plants but you might be surprised just how much you already know. You may well scratch your head if asked the question 'What is Galanthus?' But if someone asked you instead to describe the snowdrop you would hardly be worried...they are one and the same plant!

There is even a little excitement in finding out the names of plants and what they mean. Many of the names given to plants sound Greek or Latin but are often horticultural version of the name of the person for whom the group of plants has been named.

★ The camellia, those lovely evergreen shrubs and trees, were named for Georg Josef Kamel (1661-1706) a Jesuit pharmacist who was also a botanist and a writer working in the

Philippines.

★ Copernica, a palm tree, is named for Copernicus, the great Polish astronomer, physician, ecomomist and theologian who lived from 1457-1543 and whose theories changed the whole face of astronomy.

★ Narcissus, part of the daffodil group, is for the beautiful Greek youth who became so entranced by the reflection of his own good looks that the gods turned him into a flower.

★ Delphinium is from the Greek for Dolphin.

★ Gladiolus is Latin for a small sword—and indeed the leaves do look just like a sword.

★ Tulip may have come from the Turkish word for *tulnana*, a turban.

So don't be put off by a name; look at it and see how easy it really is to say and then check it out and you will find that it very probably has a romantic story behind it. If that doesn't interest you just check and you will find that there is very likely a simple and popular name for the same plant.

As we go through this book you will find that I will be using the popular names first but behind them I will give the name that you might have to look out for if you are buying a plant or a packet of seeds. They are easier to find under their 'official' name.

But flowers are not popular just for their names or the romance associated with them. Their beauty can belong to anyone; they are easy to raise; they brighten life with their colours, their shapes and their smells. And you need nothing more than a pot on a windowsill or just in a place at home where you can have your own secret garden. Always remember that this is your garden...the place where you can grow what you like without any help or hindrance from anyone.

The wonderful thing about most plants is that they only need a little simple care and attention. Take any plant and give it food and water, light and air and a little bit of love and you will have the makings of your own successful garden—tiny, large, even in a pot as small as a yogurt jar!

Buying plants today is so much easier than it ever was, but the great fun and excitement is finding the seeds from plants and growing them on. Or taking a small cutting and watching it as it puts out its own roots and makes a new living plant.

It is even quite a simple operation to breed your own plant—yes, a completely new type of flower that no one else in the world has! And again all you need is the tiniest space!

Let us go now and enjoy the excitement of growing things.

How a seed becomes a plant

Which came first — the plant or the seed? It is one of those highly debatable questions but if you could go back millions of years you would find the answer.

The first plants that colonised the earth arrived over 400 million years ago. These were moss and fern types without flowers and they cast off spores which reproduced and continued the plants' existence. These spores can lie dormant for thousands of years but their survival rate is low because they carry no food store. Eventually the plants underwent a change and began to reproduce seeds as well as spores—which just about provides the answer to which came first the plant or the seed. Yes, the plant came first.

Nowadays the way a seed becomes a plant is very simple to see and watch.

A seed blown by the wind falls from the parent plant on to the ground and there germinates as the soil and water break down the outer coat.

A tiny little root bursts out of the seed and burrows into the soil to find water and nutrients. Then two little ears, called cotyledons, appear, followed by a stem which will be the bearer of light to the plant. Meanwhile the root spreads as the stem grows and more and more tiny hair roots are pushed around in the soil to find more food and water. As the plant ages so those first early little ear-like leaves die away and the real plant leaves take over.

You can see this work for you in your garden or on a windowsill. Take any seed … from a conker to a tiny primrose seed … and you can watch this wonder of nature growing up in even the smallest container.

1

Is There a Nut in the House?

Waiting weeks or even months to see the results of seeds that you have sown is no fun—and unless you have great patience it can be a bore! But there is a whole world of easy-to-produce plants right there in your own home already—or if they are not there they are easy to find.

If there is a nut or a pip or even the top of a carrot in the house then you have the makings of a plant. If there is something exotic like a pineapple top, an avocado seed or a Kiwi fruit than you can have more fun than you ever anticipated right there on the windowsill.

So here is a whole wonderland for you to enjoy. For everything from flowers to fruit to the start of a giant tree you need little more than an empty yogurt jar or an egg box to get them started.

When you are working on your growing experiments do not spread yourself out on the floor...that is the easiest way to have someone knock over all your work and possibly ruin the project. No, get a table, cover it well with paper and they set out all the things you will need like cartons or pots. Yogurt cartons are very useful but remember to make three or four holes in the bottom to allow unnecessary water to soak away. Next you will need some soil or compost (all the details for this appear in chapter 7), plus, of course, the seeds you are going to use. As simple as that.

So let us begin with the pips and the pieces...

Avocados are without a doubt the most spectacular and easy of all plants to get growing. There are two types, a rounded one from America, and the pear-shaped one from the Middle East, which is the easier of the two to grow. If your family doesn't use avocados then ask the greengrocer to hold on to one that has possibly gone over-ripe and cannot be sold in the normal way.When you get one of these large stones soak it at least for a day in warmish water. Fill a narrow-necked jam jar full of water and if your seed does not sit naturally on top then balance it with some toothpicks which can actually pierce the sides without damaging growth.

Put the seed away in a warm, dark place and keep the jar topped-up with water. After a short time you will see a root appearing at the base and a shoot emerge from the top. All this may only take days but some seeds are stubborn and could take weeks.

When the roots have developed in the water the plant can be transplanted to a compost-filled pot. It will grow fast once it becomes established but in order to have a really good bushy plant the top of the main stem should be snipped off when it has reached a height of about 15 cm (6 ins). If it grows too fast and too big for its first pot then change it into a larger pot—but be careful, try not to disturb the roots too much when you are moving it. The way to do this is to have the new pot ready with some additional compost; then knock out the plant and place it immediately into the new pot. Fill around the sides with more compost. It will need regular watering and feeding with a liquid fertiliser.

Sometimes a seed will not germinate. The signs are when the water in the jam jar becomes cloudy and dirty. You will just have to throw this effort away and begin again.

Oranges and *lemons* — next time you eat an orange or a tangerine or a clementine don't throw away the pips. Hold them for planting and they might well surprise you! Any pips from citrus fruit can be used to experiment with and while you will not get fruit like the one from which you got the seed, they could well produce little fruits that are quite attractive. Plant the pips in a damp compost in any sort of pot or yogurt carton. The depth of planting should be about 13 mm (1/2 in). The pot should then be placed in a warm dark place (the airing cupboard or in a safe place in a boiler room). Within a month there should be little shoots appearing and then the pots should be brought into the light. The plants can be potted on when they reach about 7.5 cm (3 ins). The plants will grow quite happily even outside in a normal sunny spot but will be killed by frost. They will, of course, perform wonderfully well if you can keep them in a sunny spot by a window.

Pineapple tops can be grown to make super houseplants. You just cut the top off the pineapple and leave a fleshy piece underneath. Leave it to dry for a day or so and then get a large pot filled with compost (the pot should be wide enough to allow you to

water the soil and not just the plant piece.)
Cover the fleshy part with compost and then
find a sunny, warm and bright spot to allow
the plant to grow. It will need constant
watering and a constant spray on the leaves
will give it a better chance to root. When you
see some new green shoots emerge you will
know that it has rooted. Don't expect it to
produce pineapples but don't be too surprised
if, one day,you see tiny fruit on the now well
growing plant!

Carrot, beetroot and parsnip tops — While a
plant grown from a pineapple top will grow
into a long lasting house plant the same

Acorn

Avocado Pear

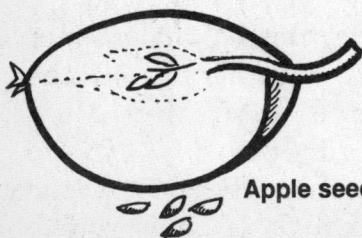

Apple seeds

Pine seeds

cannot be said for vegetable tops. But they make great little forests of growth and after all they are only the scraps left over from the vegetable peelings. As long as there is a piece of the vegetable (about 13mm — (1/2in) left under the green top there will be room for the plant to grow. You can plant them in a carton or pot with compost or just lay them in a pan of water. You will have them sprouting in very quick time.

Mustard'n'cress — Here now is something that will surprise, delight — and feed you! These are just about the fastest growing seeds that you get anywhere. They don't ask

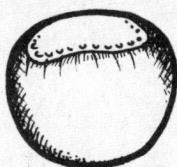

Conker

Hazel nut

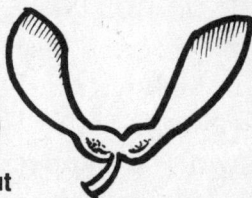

Sycamore 'Helicopter'

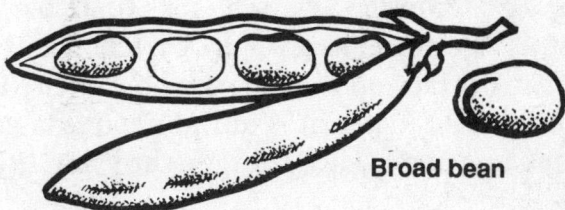

Broad bean

anything more for success than something damp on which to grow—this can be kitchen towels, blotting paper or even a damp cloth. If you are using kitchen paper towels just fold them into a thickness of about three layers, place them on a plate or in a baking-tray and then moisten well. Plant the seeds on top.Within days you will have your own little world of growing vegetable that you can snip and use in a salad or sandwich. And it will be all your own work.

But there is also great fun that you can have with the same mustard and cress seed. Draw a house on a piece of paper and then arrange a lawn in front of the house. Damp the paper (with should be about treble thickness) thoroughly and just plant the seeds where you have the lawn marked.

Draw a cat and fill her tail with seeds; draw a clown's face and give him mustard and cress hair. There are hundreds of bright ideas that will give you endless fun and a chance to use your imagination. Think for instance of putting the seeds in a yogurt carton and then painting a face on the side of the carton! The result could be quite fun...but don't ever forget just how tasty the mustard and cress can be!

Bean sprouts which you would find in a Chinese restaurant can be grown in much the same way except that they have to be kept in the dark as they grow. A simple way to grow them is to soak some seeds in cold water overnight. This makes them swell and easier to germinate. Rinse them under the cold tap and dry. Put a layer of seeds—about 2.5 cm (1 inch) in the bottom of a jam jar and fill with water. After a minute or so drain the water away. The same results can be achieved by placing the seeds in a sieve and washing them gently under the cold tap. Place a piece of muslin over the top of the jar and put it in a warm airing cupboard. Repeat the water trick with them each day and within a week they will be well sprouted. Cook and eat them as they become greenish and are still young. Look for them as 'mung beans' in the seed catalogues but do make sure that the seeds you buy are suitable for indoor planting and have not been treated with any sort of chemicals ... always ask for advice in a gardening shop or centre.

Beans or peas in a jam jar — This will give you a good demonstration of how seeds germinate and you can actually watch it

happen. Place a rolled up piece of blotting
paper so that it fits tightly around the inside
of a jam jar and then add about 2.5 cm (1 inch)
of water. The paper will soak up the water.
Then place a couple of seeds between the glass
and the the moist blotting paper. Do not allow
the paper to dry out. It can be kept moist by
just adding a little water to the bottom of the
jar regularly. If you watch it every day you
will see the seed grow and grow. It will put out
a straggly green shoot but this would need to
be transferred to compost as water would not
provide enough nutrients for it to live.
However it could be planted in the garden
where it should grow on.

Nuts, seeds and conkers — Most of the trees
and plants that we have in the garden can be
grown from seed—although it will take a
lifetime to see a decent result from a very slow
growing acorn or even from a conker.
However hazel nuts, acorns, sycamore
'helicopters' and even pine cones all provide
material for the enthusiastic planter. The
time to collect most of these is the autumn.
They can be planted into pots of compost and
soil and then left outside to over-winter. Mice
and squirrels love seed so you should protect
the pots with netting. Bring them inside in

early spring and very soon you will see the first small trees emerging. When they reach about 30 cm (1ft) high they should be transplanted outside because they are trees and will be happier in the outdoor environment—anyway they do not make very attractive house plants. You can, however, keep them indoors for years by pruning back the new growth and the roots in a very famous method known as *bonsai*. There are many books available on this ancient Oriental art.

Into this category of growing you can add apple and pear seeds but don't expect these to produce fruit for you as most cultivated apple trees have to be grafted on to wild stock before they can effectively fruit.

Pines usually hide their seeds deep in the cones. Only when the cones open up are the seeds ready to be produced. You can get them to open by placing them in a warm place and then shake out the seeds. These will grow into quite useful little trees.

Kiwi fruit — This famous New Zealand fruit (also known as a Chinese gooseberry) produces lovely house plants. Take some seed (from a very ripe fruit) and dry it out. Plant it in the usual type of compost and keep it warm and moist. When the seedlings emerge they can be transplanted on and within a year will have made quite handsome plants. But again don't expect fruit.

A strange plant

The Welwitschia grows only in a tiny part of the Southern Africa desert. It lives for 100 years but in all that time only produces two leaves!

However as they age these leaves become torn by sand and wind and provide the appearance of many more. As the leaves are produced from the base of the plant the shredded remains are constantly renewed.

2

Growing from Seed

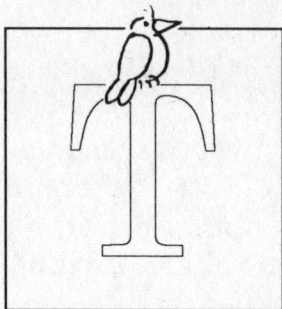

he fastest growing garden flower seeds that you can get are annuals...which are simply plants that flower and die within the one year. You put the seeds down in April and by June you will have flowers. Leave them alone and they will spread their seeds on the ground and some will go on reproducing themselves for ever—but on the arrival of the first frosts the plants themselves will begin to die down!

Annual seeds are very easy to buy...most stores will have racks of the brightly coloured packs but do make sure that you know what you are buying because there are many, many other flowers seeds on sale that will not grow quite as quickly as the annual. Popular ones like the pansy or the polyanthus-primula need caring for over a year—but that in its own way is exciting as you can watch in detail the development of the plant from a tiny seed right through to flowering and then reseeding. You can do this on the windowsill or in any sheltered, warm and sunny spot.

Let us look at some types of seed which will give you success:

Some of these that I am about to mention are annuals, others fit into different categories and will need different treatment...but all of them will give exciting times as they reproduce. Some packages are quite expensive but if you had to buy the plants instead you would see just how inexpensive it is to raise them yourself.

Take the lovely primula (a highly coloured and fragrant relative of the primrose and the polyanthus—indeed the dividing line between them is very very thin). One plant alone will cost about £1—but for that price you can get enough seeds to produce up to 100 plants! All it needs is a little TLC—a substance that gardeners mention often and which simply means Tender Loving Care...it is what plants thrive on.

Here are the rules for seed planting—as well as the names of some of the plants that are certain to give satisfaction.

★ The time to plant these seeds is generally in spring, from March to April.

★ Annuals can be planted outdoors then and left to flower in the same place. When they begin to grow you will have to thin them out and then cover the beds or rows with twigs or wire to keep the birds off. There is a huge range of annuals available but look out specially for these. Remember that the first name is the popular name and the next name (if necessary) is the one that you will find on the seed packet.

Cornflower—once considered to be a weed; now a lovely flower in many colours.

Corn Cockle (Agrostemma)—a flower that once decorated those old-fashioned gardens and now often regarded as a weed but a lovely flower for cutting. Butterflies love it too.

Corn Marigold (Calendula) —all you need is a pinch of seed in the spring and in ten weeks there will be masses of yellow daisy-like flowers. This is the old-fashioned type but today there are many different types of marigolds, also known as calendula, is many different shades of orange and yellow.

Poppy (Papaver) —You may think of poppies

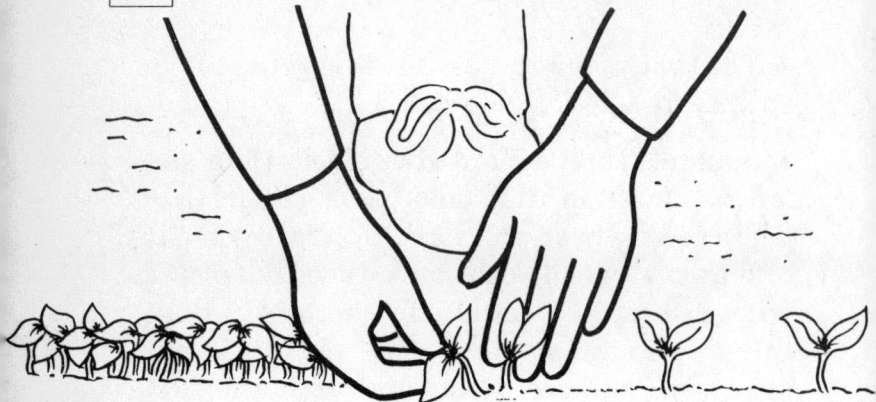

Thinning out

as just red/purple flowers but today you can find them in all colours. Do not transplant them—just leave them to grow where you have planted the seeds. And they will self-seed for years.

Just some others that you might like to try:

Alyssum—little cushion for the front of a border.

Baby Blue Eyes (Nemophilia)—a low growing and pretty flower (in other colours than blue too) but you should remember that is doesn't like being disturbed.

Clarkia—one of the easiest to grow, but plant the seeds where you want it to grow as it does

not like being disturbed.

Love-in-a-mist—lovely in all colours but blue is still the prettiest.

Nasturtium (Tropaeolum)—this orange-yellow flowering plant will spread anywhere it is allowed to go.

Poached Egg Flower (Limnanthes) — once you get this one to grow it will be hard to get rid of it as it re-seeds easily. And it is exactly like a poached egg!

Straw Flower (Helichrysum)—one of the everlasting flowers that you can save for winter; cut them before the flowers open fully. For details on preserving flowers see page 112

They are just some of the annuals which can be sown direct from the package into your garden. There are many other wonderful plants that can be grown the same way but they do need different care. Among them are the half-hardy annuals and they require different treatment to get them to grow to their very best, although they too can be planted outside once the ground has really warmed up and they will also flower that summer. But for the best results follow the following rules:

To begin with the seeds should be planted in a special container. The seeds will need protection under a plastic cover or a sheet of glass on the windowsill.

★ Seeds can be planted in any clean container, seed tray, seed pan or ordinary shallow flower pot. Egg boxes are quite useful if you put a drainage hole in the bottom and then plant a seed for each egg space. Yogurt cartons too can take any number of seeds and then when the plants are big enough they can be planted on individually into other containers—again the egg cartons are very useful for this. Mark the names of all seeds clearly on the containers before you plant them...no, you will not remember correctly which has been planted where, when you have finally planted two or three lots!

★ The best soil for seeds can be purchased in quite small packs in any store but if you cannot get that you should mix some fine garden soil with a little sand and some peat moss. This, when dampened, will get the seeds started.

★ Firm the compost into the container with your fists or a piece of board. The compost should be moist but not wet when you are sowing the seeds.

★ Scatter the seeds thinly. This can be tedious but the more space you can give them the fewer plants you will lose later on when you have to transplant them. The smaller seeds can be mixed with sand for equal distribution.

★ Cover them with a very fine layer of soil. There are many different types of seeds... very fine ones need not be covered at all ... but most will need a slight covering and must always be in full contact with the soil. The bigger the seed the more depth it needs. Think of giving seeds covering of about twice their own size. When you are firming them in make sure that they do not stick to the firming board or to your hand.

★ You will need to cover the tray with a sheet of glass and put some dark brown paper on top. Even a transparent sheet of plastic will do. And if they are placed on the window sill start them on the less sunny side, moving them over as they begin to grow. Keep them at a steady warmth if you can and wipe the glass clean fairly frequently.

★ As soon as they have started to germinate the seedlings will need light, so take away the paper and prop the glass up for a day or so, after which it can be removed altogether. They should then be moved into the full light gradually and the soil kept damp—but not soaking wet.

★ They will take a few days to grow stronger but when the first true leaves have arrived you can transplant the seedlings into other containers filled with potting compost, which again you can buy in small bags. Very gently then lift the seedlings by the leaves; do not lift them by the stems as these can be very easily damaged. The little plants should be given room to develop and left in the shade until they have settled into their new quarters.

★ Next you have to harden them off before

planting out in the garden. Move the container to a cool room or a garden frame where the plants can be be hardened off. Gradually move them outdoors for a few hours during daylight. About a week before you need to plant them out, leave them outdoors all the time.

Raising plants from seeds is far simpler than words can tell. Try it and see. Buy just one packet of seeds and you will be setting out on one of the great delights of nature.

Here now are some of the interesting plants that you can grow by the method I have just described. They will grow very quickly when planted outside—but there is nothing to stop you growing them on to full size in a pot in the house. Unless I mention it they will all need a sunny, warm spot in good soil.

Busy Lizzie (Impatiens) Everyone knows that this is the busiest little plant of the summer and will grow anywhere, especially in a shady, damp spot.

Cock's Comb (Celosia) A tender but lovely plant of plumes or crested heads in bright shades of red, yellow and orange...and just like a cock's comb. It makes an excellent cutting flower.

Floss Flower (Ageratum) Heads that are like powder puffs, lots of flowers that are long-lasting. Need shelter and lots of water. Best known for blue flowers but there are other colours too.

Love-lies-bleeding (Amaranthus). Long tassles made up of lots of tiny blooms. Most are red, there is one with green tassles. Does not need rich soil.

Petunia — If you want to name the most colourful plant among these, this would surely be a candidate...flowers come in all colours from white to mauve. Make great plants for a hanging basket or a window box. Do not like very wet conditions and need a little shelter from rain.

Painted Tongue (Salpiglossis). The strangest mixture of colours in velvety, funnel shaped flowers — you will find gold on purple, red on yellow and yellow on red. They are leggy and may need some support to grow well

Pansy (Viola). Not really a half-hardy annual but seeds are treated in the same way. Wonderful for bedding, edging or window boxes. They cut well too...but beware slugs also like them!

Primula, primrose and polyanthus. There is a

great range of plants in this one section and from a packet of seed you can get a wonderful selection—try the 'Pacific' or the 'Goldlace' strains. When you have a few plants growing in your own garden or in a pot you can leave on some of the flowers so that they go to seed. Collect the seed from the dead flower heads, dry it and then sow it the same as you would any bought seed. You can do this with just about every plant in this group.

Snapdragon (Anthirrhinum). Yes—it does look like a dragon's mouth when you open the bloom! But for this type ask for the old fashioned strain that will be known on the packet as Anthirrinum Majus.

Spider Plant (Cleome). Here is an exotic and very scented flower that is just like a spider or fisherman's fly.

Statice or Sea Lavender (Limonium) The everlasting flower that has a papery touch about it. Easily dried for use all the year round. All colours.

Treasure Flower (Gazania) It is a treasure in that its daisy-like flowers are bright and showy during the day but close up at night. If you live near the seaside this is the plant to grow.

What they need to grow

Plants ask for very little from the gardener and to get them growing at the very best you only have to give them:

> Light
>
> Water
>
> Food
>
> Air
>
> Warmth
>
> And a little bit of love

If you stop and think about those needs you will realise that it is exactly what every human needs for a happy existence. Plants deserve the same.

There are some places in the world where plants will not grow:

★ In the heart of a desert where water is not available

★ On mountain-peaks which are constantly covered in snow because there is virtually no warmth there

★ Deep in the heart of a cave because they will not get light there

But there is not a spot in any sort of garden where you will fail to find a plant to suit...because our climate is perfect for just about every plant on this earth.

3
Special Flowers

part from the annuals and the half-hardy annuals mentioned in the previous chapter there are some other special flowers that could fit in with the same sort of treatment but because they are so special they deserve a little more attention paid to them.

Sweet Pea —One of the loveliest of summer's flower, delicate with a wonderful fragrance. It will go on happily providing lovely bouquets for months.

No one knows where sweet pea really came from. The first mentions of them are in writings from about 1700 but since then they have become one of the best loved of all annual flowers.Their official name is *Laythrus* but most catalogues call them by their common name so you will never have any trouble finding lots and lots of different types of seeds.

The mixtures are probably best as they will give you very colourful selections. But eventual plant sizes must be watched as you can get sweet pea that grows from a height of 1.8 m (6 ft) down to 45 cm (18ins).

The taller types will need to be staked or attached by a string to a wall or a fence while the lower growers are dwarf enough even to make a very unusual and colourful window-box.

The sweet pea is a hardy annual but it benefits greatly from a little special attention.

The seeds have a very tough coating so they will need a little help in germinating. Some people just soak them for a short while in water, slightly warm water is best, while others chip at each seed with a nail file and make the surface weaker so that the plant can fight its own way out.

It is best to start the seeds indoors; again your yogurt pots come in useful for starting them off. You will get about 25 seeds in each packet and you should make use of them all because they are large enough to handle easily.

Plant them in a good seed compost and

when they have grown on you may need to stake them to keep them growing straight. When risk of frost is past you can plant them outdoors.

If you want to plant them outdoors wait until the weather warms up in early spring and then sow seeds about half-an-inch deep in a rich soil. When the plants emerge they will do best in full sun and remember that they will need constant watering. They also need regular feeding—some liquid fertiliser every 10-12 days will keep them growing well.

The biggest problem will come from slugs, which if allowed to run riot will gladly eat all your plants away.

Support the young plants with twigs which will encourage climbing. About three to six weeks later main supports to a height of some 1.8 m (6 ft) should be put in place. This support can be provided by canes or plastic netting.

Bushy plants can be achieved by pinching out the top growth when a height of about 10 cm (4 ins) is reached. They will benefit from a good mulch in May—this will retain moisture during dry spells but the plant will still need watering.

Cut the flowers with a scissors when the

bottom bloom on each stem shows full colour.
Make sure that the dead flowers are always
cut away as this will encourage the plant to go
on blooming.

There are many, many varieties of sweet
pea available and among the lower-growing
ones you should look for 'Little Sweetheart',
'Snoopea', 'Peter Pan' or 'Bijou'. If you want to
make a lovely mix also plant some Clarkia,
Candytuft and the blue cornflower with them.

Chrysanthemum—The chrysanthemum is
said to have begun its life in China round
about the year 500 B.C. and today it is among
the most popular of flowers world wide. There
is a huge variety of chrystanthemums
available and they can be grown just about
anywhere from a rock garden to a window
box, from a general border to a greenhouse.
They come in annual form which are easily
grown from seed sown in February (the
Charm and Cascade varieties for instance), or
as herbaceous plants such as the Shasta
Daisy, but they are probably best known for
their autumn flowers.

Make sure that you check well the eventual
size of the plant and the type of flowers it
produces before you buy it ... some can carry
bouquets of flowers while others will give very

tall, leggy plants that will need staking.

Chrysanthemums know the sort of home they like best—it should be sunny, with a soil that holds its moisture but in not water-logged. They like the soil to be rich with manure.

Water them well in dry spells and feed them regularly (every 2 weeks). Slugs and birds will cause the main trouble so you will have to find ways to deter these from enjoying your plants more than you do!

The plants can be divided in the autumn to give you a whole host of new ones. Carefully dig up the clump and you will find that the

new plants are all around it. Gently pull these off individually and replant them, making sure that you give them room to expand. You should be able to get about 10 to 15 plants from a normal clump of chrysanthemums.

The same message goes for these as for most other plants—do not let the flowers die on the plant

Lupinus—The lupin is one of the great flowers for a garden.They flower without too much trouble and if left alone will go on and on re-seeding themselves and making bigger clumps just about every year.

Not everyone loves them for their re-seeding habit. In New Zealand some years ago a nursery that was growing large numbers of Russell Lupins was flooded and seeds were carried long distances. The result is that today they have become a pretty sight—but also an environmental hazard as they block up streams and rivers with a constant supply of new plants.

The man who gets the credit for the modern lupin is George Russell, who selected many seeds from his allotment and improved the strain enormously in the 1930s.

Lupins are quick growing, tolerant of most conditions and can be bought in a wide range of colours. They grow in large, densely packed masses of bloom and will survive if the slugs and mildew can be kept at bay. They can be grown from seed or from basal rooted cuttings. Try a mixed selection of Russell Lupins or a packet of New Generation lupins which are regarded as being the best of modern varieties for overall flowering.

Gaillardia— This is a plant that is often called the blanket flower ... and that is a very good name because it will densely cover a large area with fiery coloured daisy-like blooms.They are excellent for cutting. To get them growing correctly they need a light, sandy soil and full sun. The stems must be cut to ground level when flowering has finished in September and the clumps should be lifted and divided to avoid deterioration. They can be grown from seeds and these will provide a variety of colours in the seedlings.

It gets its name from a French magistrate and botanist.

Gypsophila—This is the plant that is called baby's breath and will be seen often in flower arrangements or as back-up in bunches of flowers. It carries lots of tiny white flowers in thin stems with a greyish green foliage.

If you intend to give some flowers away as gifts then you must grow this one—look out for 'Bristol Fairy' which is regarded as the best with its pure white flowers.

It needs a well dug, gritty soil in a sunny position. Don't try to transplant it though once it has become established—it just hates being moved. However you can propagate them from cuttings taken in the summer.

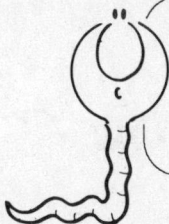

The floral code

Did you know that the floral code began hundreds of years ago and that just about every flower has some special message? What it means is that flowers can speak for you. The messages, though, may not always seem fair to the plants involved—for instance the simple, lovely butter-cup means that you consider someone ungrateful. The heather means that you are looking for solitude, you want to be on your own—and you would expect that because heather means mountains and mountains generally are places of solitude.

Some flower symbols:

Anemone	I'm foresaken
Bluebell	I'm constant
Buttercup	Ungrateful
Daisy	Innocence of youth
Fuchsia	You have great taste
Geranium	Friendship
Hyacinth	Ready for fun and play.
Ivy	Faithful friendship
Lilac	First love.
Lobelia	Watch out—evil.
Lupin	Greedy
Marigold	Grief.
Pink or Carnation	Bold.
Poppy	Consolation.
Rose	Love
Snowdrop	Hope.
Stock	Everlasting beauty
Red Tulip	I love you.

4

Bulb Growing

here can be few things more exciting in a garden than the sight of the first crocus or snowdrop pushing its way through the cold, damp winter soil to herald the approach of spring. In a few weeks they are followed by the golden waves of daffodils and then by the brighter, more stately tulips.

Once these wonderful flowers have faded many people think that this is the end of the bulb-growing season but you could have a garden almost always in flower where only bulbs grow. You will in fact be spoilt for choice. But here let us concentrate on the ways to grow spring flowering bulbs and then at the end I will give you the names of some others that can be grown later in the year.

First of all what is a bulb? Well, it has no botanical significance; it is simply meant to cover the range of bulbous plants so that it will include some corms, tubers and rhizomes (fleshy stems that creep below the surface).

Why do new bulbs seem to produce such good flowers with little or no attention? Well, the bulb that you buy in the store has already got all its energy packed inside it. And the flower is already growing inside the bulb so that it will appear almost regardless of where it is planted. But that won't happen every year unless the bulbs are treated correctly from the moment they are planted.

Often people will offer you bulbs from their gardens and they do not do as well as the ones that you bought from a store. The explanation is simple—bulbs need building up just like other plants so that they can store more energy for next year's flowers. This means that when the flowers have died away all bulbs should be given some liquid fertiliser to build up that growing store.

However there is more to it that just that— many bulbs will not produce any flowers in the following years if they have been planted in unsuitable sites.

Here are the simple ten points of good spring bulb growing:

1. Always buy the best bulbs. Big and firm

and fresh looking is what you need. All good garden centres and many stores carry boxes of bulbs with a colourful illustration on the label to encourage you to buy.

2. Don't be impulsive. You must know exactly where you are going to plant those bulbs and how many you really need. It is always better to buy from the open cartons than from pre-packs because you have a better chance of selecting the biggest and the best.

3. These cartons always give you the height and colour of the bulbs—very important if you are planting them for effect. Make sure that if you buy from a number of cartons the bulbs are put into separate bags and the names and colours and heights marked on them.

4. Don't buy bulbs with any large black patches on them or that feel even slightly soft to the touch. Shrivelled bulbs are to be avoided at all costs.

5. It is always better to buy from recognised dealers who will only sell first class bulbs that are guaranteed trouble free. Many of the very cheap offers that you see advertised are old bulbs that have been gathered from cut flower fields and will not produce the quality flowers of first class bulbs.

6. Many bulbs will not repeat their first year growth unless you have given them a good home already. A good home means deeply dug, rich, well drained soil in a bright sunny place. You would not fill a pot in the house with stony, rough soil and expect a plant to grow well so remember that the better the soil the better the flowers will be.

7. The earlier in the autumn you plant spring bulbs such as daffodil, tulip, crocus the better. They need a winter to form their root system and so be ready to give flowers in spring. Always plant them as soon after purchase as possible.

8. Snowdrops are best planted in the spring when the flowers have died down and there is still some foliage on them.

9. The depth of planting is very important. A good guide with tulips and daffodils is at least twice their own depth below soil level. This means that if a bulb is 5 cm (2 ins) from tip to base it should be planted 10 cm (4 ins) below soil level. The crocus is a special case—it needs to go down about six inches because it forms new corms (it is not strictly a bulb) on top of the old ones. If corms or bulbs are too close to the top of the soil you will find that birds pull them up so that they can get to any insects underneath.

10. Plant all bulbs in little clumps—they look better this way. Don't plant them where you expect to sow seeds in the springtime. Label them as soon as you have planted them.

Just about everything that applies to the bulbs outdoors also applies to those you intend to grow in containers or pots indoors. The only difference is, of course, that the indoor bulbs will flower much earlier because conditions are better.

One great indoor subject is the *hyacinth* which you can grow on top of a glass of water and it will flower there just taking its feeding from the water underneath. If the glass you have is too wide (a narrow necked jam jar is usually just about the right size) place cocktail sticks into the side of the bulb for balance. A warning though—the bulb will be useless after one year simply because it has only had water to keep it going so it is no good to try planting it outside.

Everyone loves to cut flowers and, of course, daffodils and tulips make ideal subjects. Cutting flowers from these bulbs does not harm their perfomance the following year but do allow the foliage to die down fully before you destroy it. This allows nutrients to go back into the bulb and builds up its strength for the next flowering season.

When the foliage has died down the tulip bulbs should be lifted and stored until they are needed again the following autumn. There are however some very special ones that should not be lifted every year—you will find out all this information on the carton labels when you are buying your bulbs.

The days when tulips and daffodils only came at 45 cm (18 ins) high have long since gone—now you can buy miniature versions of all of these. In the chapter on miniature gardens you will find a list of bulbs that will be suitable for this purpose.

Daffodils—Daffodils must be the most popular bulb of all. You will see it called a narcissus but the distinction between them is quite slight. It is called a daffodil when the centre trumpet is as long or longer than the petals.You may think of them only as yellow and creamy white flowers but there are many different types available now in colours that range from pure white to delicate pink and in blends of these colours. The growing height is from a few centimetres right up to 60 cm (2 ft) Choose a well drained and sunny position to get the best from them. Plant from August to September, the earlier the better. Give them a generous hole (recommended depth is twice the size of the bulbs) in a well cultivated piece of land. Generally they can be left undisturbed for a number of years but when the clumps get too big and provide more foliage than flowers they should be lifted and divided. Many growers do this each year when the leaves have died down. Remove the smaller bulbs from the parent—if the little bulbs are placed in an out of the way part of the garden or a nursery bed they will grow to flowering size in two or three years. Bulbs can be given some liquid fertiliser when the flowers have died down...this will build them up for the following year. Foliage should only be taken away when it has died down completely. In a dry summer the ground where the bulbs are resting should be watered deeply.

Tulip—First year tulip bulbs are undemanding and provide lovely flowers for cutting. Plant them November–December. They need good soil to show their best. Tulip bulbs will improve with being lifted every year although some will continue to increase and bloom for a number of years if left alone. They should be lifted when the foliage has turned yellow. Store the dry bulbs in a frost free place.

Every year new varieties are introduced and there is a great range of different types such as single early, double early, Triumph, Darwin, Lily-flowered, Rembrandt and Parrot—to mention just a few—and all of these have their own varieties within the groups.

Cottage Tulips, those old fashioned varieties with the egg shaped blooms that eventually open to about 5 inches wide and which come into flower from early May onwards, are probably the most popular. Their strong stems will stand up to the worst the weather can offer. If you want to try something different try some Lady Tulip *(T. clusiana).* It is what is known as a species tulip, and has greyish, grass-like foliage and slender flowers that are white, flushed or streaked, with pink.

For the dwarf tulip try *T. kaufmanniana* which blooms in March with a star-like flower. Ideal for rockery. These bulbs do not need lifting in the winter.

Other bulbs that you could consider:
Anemonae—Try the mixed de Caen strain for a lovely collection of flowers in late spring. Needs a sunny spot.

Begonias.—These are tubers and will enhance any garden or window box or hanging basket. They need a rich soil and are happiest in dappled shade.

Camassia with the strange Red Indian name of Quamash, is a simple-to-grow summer bulb with lovely starry flowers, white or blue. Happiest in a dampish, sunny spot.

Cyclamen— Everyone knows this as a potted plant with its pretty heart shaped flowers but there is a miniature version that will grow outdoors and you can buy winter, spring, summer or autumn flowering varieties.

Freesia—Bright, perfumed and colourful. There are outdoor varieties but the bulbs only last for one season.

Gladiolus—There is a huge range of this wonderful flower which comes in many shapes, sizes and colours. You plant in spring to flower in summer and them they must be lifted and stored. Needs a lot of water in dry weather. They are wonderful for cutting and for this purpose they should be planted alone where they can be staked and treated separately

Iris—Those big tall iris grow from rhizomes—the bulb ones are smaller and are for the border of the miniature garden.

Star of Bethlehem (proper botanical name is *Ornithogalum*)—here is a beautiful pot plant for spring gowing. Its white flowers have a greenish centre. There are outdoor ones and the one for low growing (about 15 cm - 6 ins).

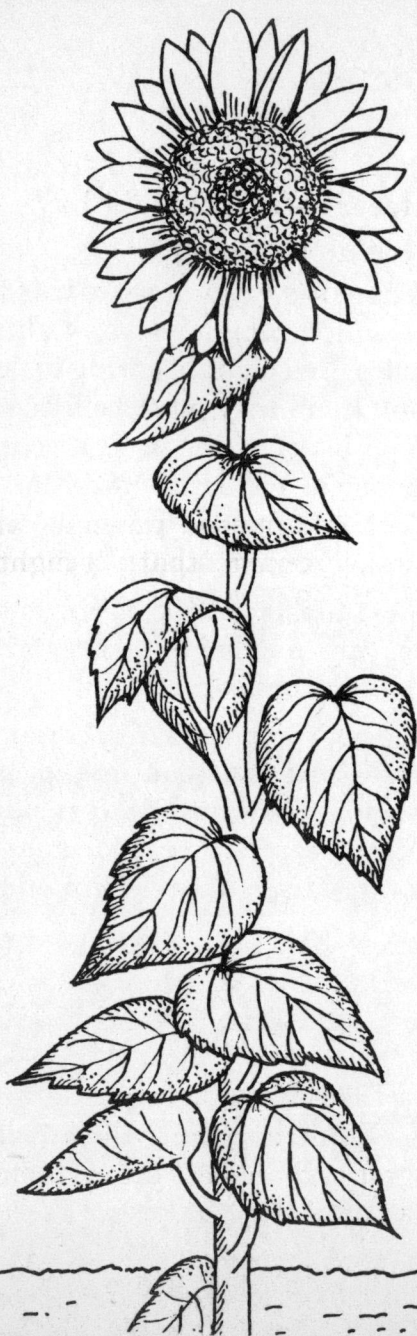

5

Grow A Giant

Can you imagine an onion that weights 9 lb. 3 oz?
Or a leek that measures 320.29 cu. ins?
Or a sunflower that reaches 23 ft.6½ ins—almost to the eaves of a two storey house?

Yes, it does stretch the imagination but it has happened. The big onion broke the world record in 1988 for a Yorkshire man, Kevin Foster, and the leeks broke the world record in the same year...the first time ever that the 300 cu ins barrier had been broken. The sunflower record was set in 1976 by a Devonshire man, Mr. Frank Kelland, who died in 1988.

Every year new records are being tackled—and broken—as gardeners pit their wits against the biggest and the best before them.

Now you may not aim for these record

breaking wonders but it would be great fun to grow a real giant wouldn't it? And the surprising thing is that it isn't really all that hard once you are prepared to give the project your dedication.

The best way to tackle something like this is to have a little competition—between your school friends or even within your own family. You could get the head of your school to organise a giant sunflower competition—and the cost would be negligible. You may well find that newspapers or magazines in your area sponsor competitions for the year's biggest sunflower—certainly some of the gardening papers do.

One of the champion varieties likely to grow a super sunflower for you is Giant Single which can be bought from Mr Fothergill's seeds for about 46p for a packet of 50!

Think of all the fun that those 50 seeds spread throughout your pals would generate. Other biggies are Russian Giant and Tall Single.

These then are the sunflowers that create all the annual competition to see who will raise the tallest golden flowered sunflower in the country, and you can do it with just a little bit of dedication to give you real flower power!

So let us look at a plan of campaign to get this giant in your garden.

First remember that there are sunflower seeds (they are called *Helianthus*) which will only produce plants that grow to 60 cm (2 ft) high and others that grow in clumps quite unlike the great sunflowers. So look for *Helianthus annuus* and then find out from details on the pack if you have indeed one of the Giant types.

Select a sunny spot in your garden where there is good soil and also shelter. Sun is very important to get the flower to reach to the skies but the shelter is even more so. Winds and heavy rain can cause all sorts of disasters for your sunflower so try to have them growing where there is some natural protection or where you can give it some artifical help. I once knew a group of children who wanted to grow the record sunflower and they took turns caring for it. They even went as far as to arrange for one of the fathers to provide a special cover that could be dropped down like a blind in front of it when the wind and rain came.

They did not do too badly either—the flower was up to over 4 m (13 ft) when the covering slipped and broke the flower! You do not want that to happen to you and there was really no need for such a covering—plants are made to withstand normal summer hazards and you can always help the really tall flowers by giving them some sort of stake that will help them beat off summer storms. But do not despair if you cannot manage this; the sunflower stem is as strong as a young tree!

Plant the seeds about 2.5 cm (1 in) deep in the soil in April. Plant them in the spot where they will grow—this is important because they do not transplant well. They will be flowering from July to September.

It is important that you give the emerging plant all the help you can afford to get it to giant size. This means regular watering and feeding with a liquid fertiliser—set yourself a date every week when you will give it the fertiliser. Make the date and even the time the top tasks of the week...and the sunflower will respond. But it also needs water—often more than once a week. Don't just dribble a few drops of water on the ground. A good deep watering on a regular basis is important— especially if there is a dry spell. If your plant gets checked because of drying out you will never get it to reach giant status.

There are lots of other ideas for

competitions that you can arrange—the longest carrot, the highest runner bean, or even the heaviest onion...but they take a lot more expertise and know-how than the sunflower. Start with the sunflower and then—maybe next year—you can try for one of the other records!

Record breakers!

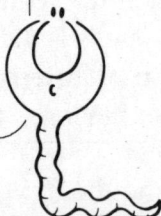

The Guinness Book of Records has many, many entries about flowers and plants.

They show that the oldest thing in the plant world is a clone of the cresote plant which may be 11,700 years old!

The smallest flowering plant is the floating aquatic duck-weed which is only 0.2mm 1/50 of an inch in length and 0.2 1/125 of an inch in width.

The fastest growing plant was a *Herperogucca Whipplei* of the Lilac family which grew 3.65m 12ft. in 14 days in an Abbey on the Isle of Scilly.

The longest daisy-chain, made in 7 hours, was one of 1380.5 m, 529 ft, at the Museum of Childhood, Sudbery, Derbyshire in June 1981. The team making it is limited to 16.

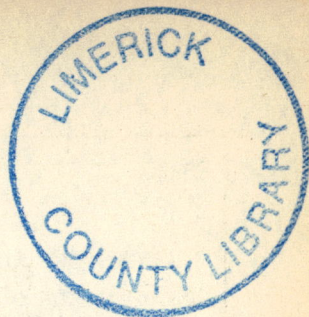

6

The Queen of the Garden

ow would you like to have Cinderella in your garden? Or the Seven Dwarfs? Or Peek-a-Boo? Or Little White Pet? Or Easter Morn? Or Fire Princess? Or Hula Girl? Or New Penny?

Wonderful names, aren't they? And they do bring some lovely images with them too. These are just a few of the huge range of small roses that are available today for gardens.

For thousands of years people have been growing roses. Cleopatra in ancient Rome covered her banqueting floor with rose petals; Empress Josephine sent men throughout the world to collect the different roses and bring them back to her French palace of Malmaison. No other flower really touches the magnificence of the rose and it well deserves its title of Queen of all Flowers.

The rose today comes in just about every colour (except true blue and full black) and in every size—from a couple of inches high to a tree towering 40 ft. The most recent full register of roses showed that there were some 17,000 known varieties in the world!

The most recent introduction to the world of the rose has been that of miniature plants. These have been perfected to the stage where exact images of the perfect flower are reflected in rose blooms that are often no more bigger than a baby's thumb nail! Plants too can be found among these little ones that have, unlike most of their big brothers, very few thorns.

And these little roses are excelling in one other area too—they are almost as easy to root as either the geranium or the fuchsia. You can take a small finger length cutting from them and treat it exactly as detailed in chapter 7 and within a few months you will have another plant exactly the same as the parent from which you took the cutting.

The miniature rose is one of the most adaptable plants that you can find. It will happily grow in a rockery, in a border, in a bed, in a pot, in window boxes or even in hanging baskets. It comes in lots of lovely colours—red, pink, orange,yellow, lavender, purple,white, green and combinations of all these colours.

In recent years the miniatures have come along so fast that in some parts of the world they are even outselling the big and much older roses. But only ten years ago they were being dismissed as playthings.

There is evidence of the existence of miniature roses as far back as 1700 but it is only recently that rose breeders (called hybridisers) have begun to produce an almost endless stream of new varieties.

Most of the small roses that you will buy from a nursery are specially grafted for garden use but in many big stores today they are available as potted plants for indoor use. These don't have to be used just indoors— after they have flowered there they can be put into the garden or transferred to another pot and again kept indoors. Just because they come in pots doesn't mean that as soon as the flowers die down they have to be thrown out...in fact they will last for years if treated correctly.

When you go to buy your first miniature rose look for a good healthy specimen, one that is fresh and green stemmed.

If the plant is what is known as pre-packed (that is in a long sleeve-like plastic cover) make sure that the stems have not been shrivelled and dried out on a shop counter. There should not be any long white growths from the bush and it should have at least three stems. You can bring a badly shrivelled plant back to life by planting it completely under the garden soil for a couple of weeks but it will never be a really good plant.

Much the same goes for potted roses. They should be healthy, happy and green with more buds than open flowers. They should not be dried out.

By far the best way to get your miniature rose is to visit a specialist nursery and pick the best they have.

The rose that is bought in the pot should be kept under shelter until the first days of summer arrive. It should not need anything by way of feeding for the rest of the year because it will have been planted in soil that will have enough nutrients. But it will need watering; not soaked but nicely damp. And watch out for aphids—they are not all greenfly; some are actually white, brown and red! Any that arrive should not be given a welcome!

If the rose is a bare-root type (that is the one in the long plastic sleeve or straight from a grower's field) it should be planted in a pot large enough to accommodate the roots or out in the garden where it will need a sunny spot with some rich soil.

The miniature roses make perfect pot plants however and should be used for this. As window box plants they are perfect too, giving colour all season long.

Just one little plant of a miniature can be increased ten fold in the year by taking cuttings from it. The best time is late summer when you take a stem that has flowered. Cut it

to about four inches long with four sets of
leaves on it. Take off the bottom two sets, put
some rooting powder on the base and plant it
in the normal way.

They will need a good humid atmosphere so
will need a warm position, not full sun, under
cover of a plastic bag or plastic bottle (see
chapter on cuttings). They will have rooted
within three to six weeks when the covering
can be taken off.

Every year new miniatures come on the
market and these are now accompanied by
some larger minis that are called patio roses
and which are treated the same as the others.
Here are just a few of the real winners among
both of these sort of roses:

Miniatures:

Rise'n'Shine—yellow and lovely

Easter Morn—white with a bigger than
normal bloom

Kiss'n'Tell—apricot-pink shades

Cinderella—white

Fire Princess—bright red (one of the best in
this colour)

Joyce Tellian—soft pink

Stars'n'Stripes—red and white stripes

Green Diamond—a very light whitish green

Peachy White—white with just a touch of

pink
Stacey Sue—one of the smallest...a lovely
   pink
Lavender Jewel—a soft, pinky lavender
Over the Rainbow—orange-red and yellow
   bicolour
Little Artist—crimson splashed with white
Hula Girl—salmon orange
Sunblaze Roses—these come in all colours
   and are usually sold as potted plants

Patio Roses (despite their name these can be
planted anywhere in the garden but do make
lovely pot plants. Many would rate as
miniatures except that the flowers can open
quite a deal larger than the smaller plants).
Peek-a-boo—apricot and quite small flowers
Cider Cup—larger deep apricot flowers.
   Beautiful
Sweet Dream—peachy and apricot tones
   combined
Gentle Touch—soft pink
Sweet Magic—deep orange
Little White Pet—a spreading plant that is
   over 100 years of age
Little Woman—rose pink
Wee Jock—deep crimson
And what about the *Seven Dwarfs*? They
are much older roses of a type called

Compacta roses and are very healthy but
almost forgotten nowadays. You will find it
hard to purchase them.

Do you remember the names of the Seven
Dwarfs? They were Bashful, Doc, Dopey,
Grumpy, Happy, Sleepy and Sneezy.

And whatever happened to _Snow White_?
There was a little rose of this name to but it
went out of commerce and now the name has
been transferred to a full sized white rose that
was introduced to mark the 50th anniversary
of the film _Snow White_!

Do you talk to your plants?

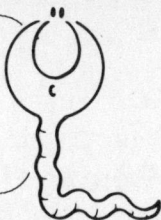

Don't laugh if you hear that someone talks to their plants, because research has shown that plants do react to people.

No one has been able to explain why this happens. Certainly a plant does not think as a human or an animal does, but it is believed that they have an in-built programme that instructs them how to react to different things! Which is why some people will grow wonderful plants and others fail.

Experiments have measured the reactions of many plants to the presence of music, noise—and people. To make these tests a machine like a lie-detector is used to record the changes in electrical resistance and changes in the way the plants grow.

Plants up pick up vibrations from people (possibly by some form of radiation) so if you want to get your plants to grow well be nice to them. Oh, yes and if you intend to play music near them make it nice gentle music! They like that better than the heavy metal sounds!

Treat your plant like you would a good friend—and you will be repaid many times over. Talk to it—it won't talk back—sing to it, be happy in its presence and your plants will grow in wonderful profusion!

7

Where Do You Get plants?

New plants are around us everywhere—just for the taking. You can get them from cuttings or from seed heads produced by flowers that have been left to form pods or from a broken piece of a tuber from a plant like a begonia.

There is great excitement in bringing home a small cutting from a holiday place or a friend's garden and seeing it root for you and eventually growing into a full sized plant.

There is a an old message among gardeners that you should never refuse to take a cutting that is offered to you. Even if you do not want it yourself you can always pass it along to a friend. But if you keep that cutting and grow it on you can increase it by huge numbers just by taking more cuttings yourself and passing them along to other friends or rooting them and giving the finished plants away.

You will soon discover that you can take cuttings from just about any plants—and any way. A cutting can be a tiny snip from the tip of a Fuchsia or a Geranium; a shoot from the base of a Delphinium or Paeony; or a cutting taken from any medium hard wood plant. All can be encouraged to grow.

Tip cuttings are very short pieces of wood that have not yet flowered and which are soft at the top and quite firm at the base.

Basal cuttings are simply from the base of the plant—usually a young shoot from around the bottom which can be pulled or cut away. Try to take some root with the piece from the base...this will give you a far greater chance of success.

Hardwood cuttings are obtained by taking off a side shoot or a short length from the main stem of a woody plant like the fuchsia.

Once you have taken the cutting here is what you do:

1. Trim off the two bottom sets of leaves that will be going under the soil. Leave some foliage intact so that the cutting can continue to breathe above ground and provide nutrients for the part under the soil.

2. Dip the base of the cutting into a hormone rooting compound. Small containers of this can be purchased in most stores and are quite inexpensive. There are two types—a powder and a liquid. If you are using the powder shake off any excess before you plant the cutting. If you don't have a hormone rooting compound try a little flour or talcum powder on the end of the stem.

3. Make a hole large enough for the cutting, using a pencil or a small piece of wood as a dibber, and insert the cutting, gently easing the soil in around it.

4. If you cannot get to plant a cutting immediately it should always be kept moist, preferably standing in just a little water.

5. Once planted, the cutting should be kept in a humid atmosphere. You can create this by covering it with a plastic bag that is held off the cutting by some twigs. Those large plastic mineral bottles make very good covers when cut in half. This covering should be able to keep the cutting moist but if there is any suggestion of it drying out give it a gentle spray of water about once a day.

6. Don't be tempted to look for roots too soon. Leave the cutting for some weeks and then if

you want to know whether it has rooted or not give a gentle tug on the cutting. If it doesn't move, then you have a success. If it does move leave it alone for a while longer.

7. If the leaves leaves begin to fall off, turn yellow or start to rot they should be lifted away from the cutting. Otherwise disease could be spread.

8. When the cutting has rooted it should be potted on into a larger container, using the utmost care not to damage any little roots that it has made. Better to keep the soil around the cutting in a ball if possible as that will save any root disturbance when you are transferring it.

9. Here is an important point. DO NOT go around pinching pieces off plants in other people's gardens. Ask any gardener for a cutting and you will be showered with them! But take them without permission and you will be in trouble!

Most plants can be rooted successfully from cuttings—and once you begin taking them you will have more successes than failures. Begin though with some simple plants that will give you almost 100% success. Among the best are fuchsias and geraniums.

**Cut clearly
just below bud/leaf joint**

**Remove the leaves from the bottom
half and dip in rooting powder**

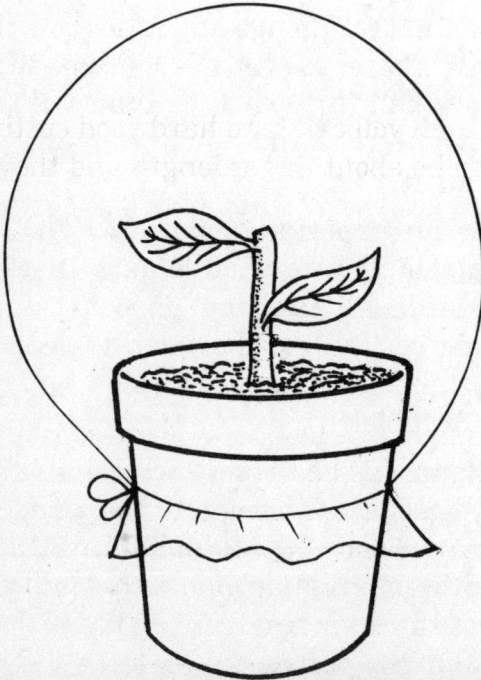

**Cover with polythene
Place in bright position**

So let us look at these plants now.

Fuchsia—This is a woody plant that is ideal for propagating. It is simple to handle and does not have any thorns or prickles that can hurt you.

You can take cuttings at just about any time and you will be amazed how quickly they will grow. In the summer the tip cuttings are by far the most successful. You will be amazed how the smallest little cutting nipped out of a growing stem, will put on roots and often give you flowers before the summer is out...but do handle them gently.

In autumn you can take hardwood cuttings. These can be about finger length and they too will make good plants quickly. While most of them only take about three weeks to root you are better off leaving the autumn cuttings in their rooting place until spring when you can move them on very successfully and they will grow into very acceptable plants.

Building up a collection of fuchsias is a very rewarding pasttime. There are hundreds of different types available in all mixes of colours and with a beautiful flower form. You will find them in white, red, mauve, violet, pink, cream, rose and combinations of these colours.

You can begin with cuttings from

neighbours and friends or you can buy rooted cuttings from many nurseries...some selling for as little as 10 plants for £4. From these ten plants you could propagate dozens more in a short space of time—they make very acceptable gifts.

There are a number of miniatures available too like 'Lady Thumb' (reddish carmine and white veined carmine), or 'Papoose' (bright red and very dark purple).

You must remember one important thing about fuchsias—there are different types that will be found under these headings: outdoor, bedding and greenhouse.

The outdoor ones are generally hardy and can be left out all year round. Bedding varieties need to be taken indoors in the winter and transferred to pots. Store in a shed with lots of light, but they do not need any food or watering until you are getting ready to plant them out in the spring. The greenhouse varieties are best treated as indoor plants but in a really good summer they can be placed outside in good sunny, warm, sheltered places.

Perargoniums (Geraniums)—Nearly everyone calls them geraniums but you may want to buy seed and this can be found under the *pelargonium* heading. But whatever you call it, the geranium is a wonderful flower. It grows happily just about anywhere and will be seen in many windows where it makes a lovely pot plant. There are special types of geraniums for hanging baskets, for bedding schemes and window boxes. If you ever go to Germany or Switzerland you will see the most wonderful window boxes full of geraniums in fine colour.

The only problem with the geranium is that it needs a frost-free growing place—so at the end of the summer plants will have to be lifted or transferred to a suitable shed or greenhouse. They should be kept there with only the tiniest amount of watering until the frosts have all passed and they can be planted out again in late spring.

For growing it needs a sandy, rich soil, good sunshine and because it is a flower from warmer and sunnier places it needs very little watering.

It is as easy as the fuchsia to raise from cuttings—either stem cuttings (any time after flowering) or non-flowered tips, usually in the early summer. By using one of these methods you can have new plants started anytime from May to September.

Take a cutting about three inches long. Again as with the fuchsia, I have always found that the non-flowered tips are best because the growth is active then and rooting is faster. The geranium has to be among the easiest plant in the world to root. Try it and see.

Other ways to get plants

In the autumn most gardeners will begin to clean up their gardens and then they often take up clumps of plants that have grown too big.

These can include all sorts of wonderful flowers and all you need to get a start is a small part of this clump.

The most successful plants to propagate in this way are those from the herbaceous border where plants are left year after year and go on multiplying at the base. You can get new plants by taking parts of the clump that is being divided or by taking a small cutting from the base when growth is beginning ... but the surest way of success if to take the piece from the broken clump.

Among the flowers that can taken in this way are Lupins, Celmatis, Delphiniums, Red Hot Poker (known as *Kniphofia*) and any of those great big flowers like the Shasta Daisy or the Oriental Poppy.

These can also be raised from seed. Most of the top producers sell packets that contain maybe hundreds of seeds although with important and new varieties you may only get six or seven seeds. However you can collect your own seed from any of these plants.

Just allow the flower to stay on the plant until the seed pod is absolutely dry. Watch it carefully and harvest it before it bursts. Leave the seeds to dry for a little while and then you can plant them in the normal way (as described in chapter 2). You will not get identical plants to the one you have taken the seed from but you will get many that are quite as good and some that may not be just as good. But remember this: they are your own seed, harvested and sown by your own hand. That makes an added excitement.

8

What Plants Need to Grow Well

oil:
Earlier in this book you will see that I have said that a plant needs food, water, air, light, warmth and little bit of love to grow well. But there was one vital ingredient missing in that list—the soil.

Nearly all plants need soil in which to grow. The roots will form a mass in the soil and hold them there against all the worst of the weather. Those roots, once anchored, will then search out for food and water in the soil.

Probably one of the greatest demonstrations of the different types of soil comes from the parable of the sower who went to sow his seeds.

As he sowed his seed he let some fall by the wayside; and the birds came and ate them up. Some fell upon stony ground where they had not much earth and they sprung up immediately because they had no depth of earth and they were scorched in the sun and because they had no root withered away. And other seeds fell among thorns and the thorns grew up and choked them. And those that fell upon good ground brought forth fruit some a hundredfold, some sixtyfold and some thirtyfold.

While there are many meanings in this parable in its simplest form it demonstrates for the gardener the need for good soil

What is soil?
Soil is just one of those everyday miracles that we take for granted. It is around us everywhere in different types and different quantities but all of it has been formed over thousands of years as rocks have broken down into tiny particles.

When these particles close together with very little air between them we have heavy clay soil; when the air pockets are more numerous you have a light sandy soil. These particles if left on their own and without some help would not provide all the food that a plant needs. There has to be an addition of humus, which is simply old leaves, roots, dead insects and animals that have rotted away over the years.

Soil also contains a number of chemicals which go to help keep plants alive. However to get into the body of the plant the chemicals need help and this is provided by water.

If water and chemicals are so important how then do plants grow in the desert? Well there are some deserts with virtually no growth but where there is growth there will generally be at least one big rainfall each year which moves the chemicals from the sand into the plant. This allows for a short but spectacular period of growth. Without that rainfall there would be very, very few plants growing in desert areas.

The soil is also the home for insects and small animals, many of which, like the earthworm, benefit the roots of plants by constantly moving the soil.If you would like to see what the earthworm really can do get some soil—sand, earth and peat moss and place them in layers in a jam jar. Cover the outside of the jars with dark paper to keep out the light and add some humus (rotted leaves for instance) on the top. Into one put some earthworms; leave one without them. In a short time you will find that while one lot of soil has not

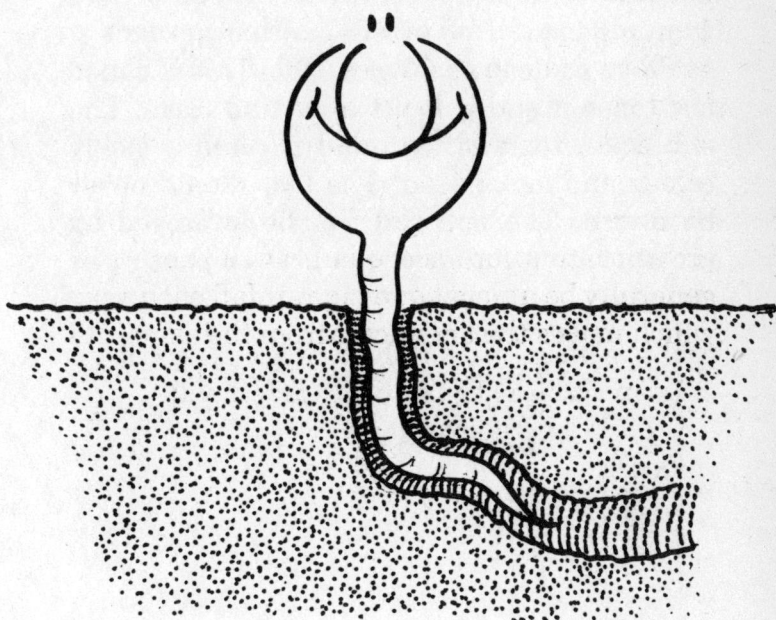

changed the soil in the jar with the earthworms has become well mixed through.

A perfect soil should be medium textured. It
will be crumbly to the touch with not too many
stones. It should also be well enough drained
to hold some water but not to become water-
logged during heavy rains. A sweet soil is
what some gardeners call it.

You will find this in gardens that have been well looked after for a number of years. It may not always be deep, sometimes it can be less than a 5 cm (2 ins) layer. In other gardens it could go as deep as 60 cms (2ft) This is called the top-soil and it looks alive and fresh. The sub soil on the other hand is often a sickly colour and looks dead. The two should never be mixed. The sub soil can be improved by incorporating manure, compost or peat moss into it.

Soil is generally described in six categories:
  Loam (that is the almost perfect soil
    described above)
  Chalk
  Clay
  Peat
  Sandy
  Stony

While most soils benefit from the addition of peat moss (in sandy soils it will help retain water and in others like clay will break up the heavy, dense mass) soils that are themselves mainly peat are often the hardest to improve. But lots of plants will still grow in peaty soil which is usually acidic and damp—these include rhododendrons and heathers.

How to make compost:
Compost will be one of the great helpers for any soil. It is made from any concoction of kitchen waste, leaves, grass clippings. In a short time this will break down and be a lovely additive to the soil. It can be made in a bin or wood receptacle which must have holes so that air can penetrate at all levels.

It should also be well mixed so that there is not too much grass or leaves in one place. A good compost heap can be made more easily in summer than in winter because the heat will encourage the various chemical changes. Water is also a vital element here ... the compost heap should never be allowed to dry out.

What fertilisers will I use?
The best of all fertilisers are manure or compost. Between them they provide lots of natural fertilisers. But these are not always easy to get these days so other fertilisers have to be used.

These fertilisers break down into two categories: organic and man made.

Organic fertilisers are obtained from many sources. Best known will be bone meal which is made from crushed bones and lasts for a long time in the soil. Wood ash is also a great provider for the soil as is dried blood.

Man-made fertilisers provide the different chemicals in a balanced way. The most important of these are:

Nitrogen—the chemical which makes plants grow, particularly their leaves and stems. Well growing and green plants are obviously getting enough nitrogen but those with yellowing, unhappy foliage are short of it. Needed most in sandy soils and rainy areas.

Phosphates—the health provider which encourages root and top growth. this will generally be needed in sandy soils. Bone meal provides this.

Potash—the essential ingredient for soft fruit and bright flower success. Essential for roses. Leaves in need of potash often turn yellow and then brown.

These will be provided in good soil as well as small amounts of iron, sulphur, magnesium, calcium, zinc and copper all of which are necessary for a successful plant.

Because we ask so much from our soils these days the addition of some man made fertiliser is vital. A well-fed plant will be healthy for most of the summer.

If you are using any of these fertilisers,

natural or man made, please do make sure
that you:
★ Wear gloves. Any of the chemicals getting
into the smallest cut on your hands can be
dangerous. Be careful always.

★ Use only the amount specified on the packets of fertiliser.

★ Do not allow fertiliser to fall on the foliage of
any plant. If you do the foliage will probably
burn and die.

★ Measure out the amount of fertiliser specified before spreading and put it into a small
matchbox to allow for easy and even distribution among the plants.

Knowing what your soil is saying
If soil in your garden is generally cold, wet and
heavy then that is clay. It will have lots of
plant foods but these will need releasing by
the generous use of compost, stable manure or
peat moss which will open it up and make it
easier to work with.

If plants produce a lot of yellow leaves you
may have a chalk sub-soil. Chalk is often
called the hungry soil so you will need to add
good amounts of manure or compost as well as
some iron and manganese every year.

If there is moss or a green slimy surface

then you know that the drainage is bad.

Soil that is gritty and fast drying is probably sandy. Again the introduction of peat moss, heavy manure or compost will improve it and help it to retain water.

A stony soil will always be that way unless all the soil is changed in the area. But once the bigger stones have been removed you will find that this is quite a productive soil.

Good clover cover will tell you that you have an alkaline soil—that is one in which most plants will grow with the exception of heathers, azeleas and rhododendrons.

Chickweed, nettles or groundsel indicate a productive and fertile soil.

If you want to check the sort of soil in your garden there are many, small and inexpensive soil test kits available that are quite good fun as well as being very helpful.

Soils for pots:
If you are growing your plants or seeds in pots or trays it is much better to purchase one of the specially packed soils that are available in every garden centre and many supermarkets.

These will make life very easy for you and provide the perfect growing medium for seeds or plants.

There are two types—soil-based and soil-less. The soil-less ones are basically made from peat moss with added nutrients and these are much lighter and easier to work with. But the heavier soil composts are better if your pots are going to sit outdoors where they will be less likely to be blown away with every little wind. Also the soil-less composts will need constant and careful watering.

Don't expect that a soil taken directly from the garden will ever provide the perfect medium for pot growing; in most cases it will need a lot of added nutrients to meet the needs of a plant growing in cramped conditions. Better by far to buy a pack of compost that will provide all this. While it is less expensive to buy in bulk only buy the amount you are likely to use within a matter of weeks...even soil composts are better when fresh.

Test for two soils:
If you doubt the ability of good soil to produce a better plant try a simple test.

Fill three yogurt jars with soil. Let one be sand, another be garden soil and a third one of the commercial composts.

Plant one plant in each of these—the plants must be identical.

After a very short time you will see the results. The plant in the good compost will take off well ahead of the garden soil one while the sand-grown one will be far behind the other two.

If you want to take this demonstration further add some liquid fertiliser when watering the plant growing in the sand—it will perk up very quickly.

9

A Miniature Garden

iniature gardens are a world all on their own. They can be just about any size from a plant tray to a whole corner of a garden. On the larger scale they can contain not only all sorts of living plants but can be made into their own landscape by mixing tiny bridges, paths, trees, statues, roadways, houses, while a small train set can add extra excitment.

How big your miniature garden is going to be depends on the space that is available as well as the time you are prepared to put into it. But the one thing to remember is that it should be miniature all over, making sure that no one feature throws the rest out of proportion.

Containers:
The best way to begin is with a tray or sink garden.

The tray garden is a very simple construction of sand fitted into a deep-sided tray or box. Into this small cuttings or branches of small plants can be inserted. These can be brought on to grow or just to present an idea of a miniature garden.

The larger seed trays are very useful for this purpose too as they are not too heavy to move around when filled and they will challenge the builder to grow the right sort of alpine plants, which are best in this situation.

By far the best way to begin is to find an old stone kitchen sink. These can often be found in builder's yards but they are becoming quite scarce as the stone sink has been replaced in recent years by the much more adaptable aluminium type. But there is nothing to stop you using a modern sink and often one that has double sinks can be very effective. They are also easier to lift. The old stone ones can be very heavy and will often need two strong men to lift them!

Sinks of any sort are always deep enough to give space for an inch or thereabout of drainage crocks, topped with the necessary soil.

Before you begin any filling remember that when you have filled the sink it will be far too heavy to move, so place it where you intend to keep it.

Apart from these smaller containers you can create a miniature garden within the garden proper by building small walls from stone or brick or even peat moss blocks.

If you want to carry the idea of the miniature garden all the way select a sunny area and you can construct a whole world of your own.

Layout ideas:

If you have a small space it is best not to try for something is too elaborate. Consider a rock garden with tiny alpine plants placed within the contours of a valley for instance. You may be tempted to include a pool but this seldom looks right in a small area. Make it look as natural as possible.

Heather

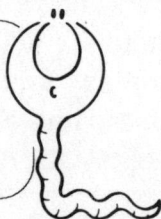

If you have a peaty garden or one that you have been told has an acid soil then you have the ideal spot to grow your spray of lucky white heather!

When you are preparing the soil a good lot of moist peat moss must be added...and this applies to the garden as well as to a planter or a pot.

The plants should be buried deeply, the foliage left resting on the ground. They need very little care and only need watering in a very dry spell.

There are so many different plants that you can have them for winter (try Silver Mist, white tipped pale pink) and for summer (try Eden Valley, white flushed purple).

When you have a couple of plants you will have no trouble making lots of new ones by taking cuttings (see page 66).

10

Growing Your Own Vegetables

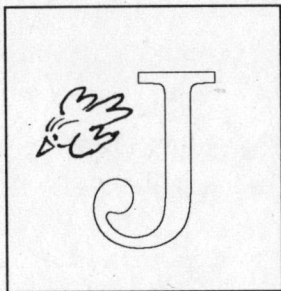

ack and the Beanstalk looks something more than just another story when you begin to grow runner beans. They really do grow as if by magic! If you want to find out how quickly they grow try this experiment.

Take some runner bean seeds in early spring and place then in soil in yogurt cartons. Leave them on a warm windowsill where they will very quickly germinate. As they grow taller in the light you will need some twigs to keep them upright. As soon as all chance of frost has passed they can be transferred to the garden where they will race away with their growth—and you will see how quickly an ordinary bean grows, never mind a supermagic one like Jack had.

If you place the plants around a frame made

in the shape of a wigwam it will amaze you
how quickly they grow to form a little house
covered in greenery ... and with some tender,
runner beans on it too!

This is one of the easiest of vegetables to
grow but there are many more that will
provide lovely, edible plants in quick time.

To get your vegetable garden ready you
must prepare the soil. This means a good dig-
ging, clearing away any signs of weeds or old
roots. Then rake it finely and within this area
make the beds that will grow your vegetables.
Always leave room to walk between the beds.

Some vegetables—like carrots, parsnip,

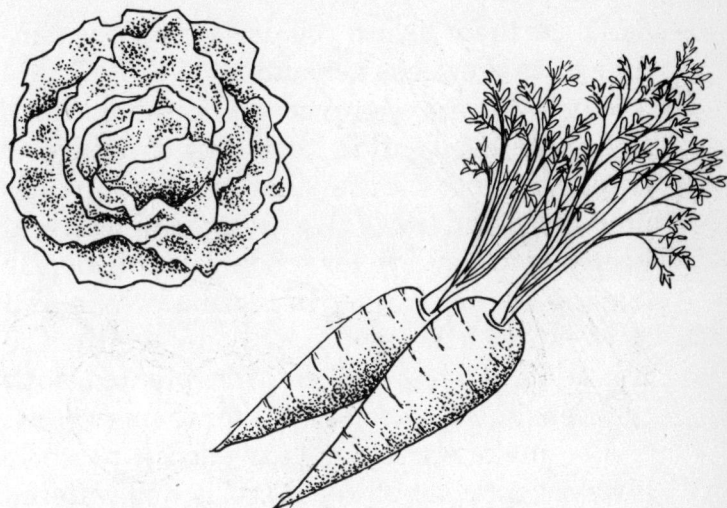

beetroot and radish must be grown on in the place where you planted the seeds. Others like lettuce can be transplanted. The trick is not to sow too many seeds. Unfortunately most vegetable seeds are small and plentiful so there is a tendency to sow them thickly. This is a mistake; sow them thinly and that will mean that you will have a much easier job—as well as less waste—when it comes to thinning them out.

The way to grow them is just the same as for annual flowers (see chapter 2). Plant them either straight into the ground or in boxes or trays. Make sure that the slugs and birds

don't get them before you do so keep a watchful eye as the seeds germinate.

When they have grown to a reasonable size
to handle easily, thin them out carefully or
transplant into the area that you have already
dug and raked finely. Water them in well and
keep a watchful eye for predators. It is no use
leaving them growing in a mass where you
have planted the seed ... they must either be
thinned out very well or transplanted with
room enough between plants for them to grow.

Also make sure that your garden patch is
always kept clear of weeds and is well watered
all summer long.

So that you will remember where you have
planted your seeds place the seed packet into
a plastic bag and fix this to a marker in the
ground. Alternatively you can make a draw-
ing in a notebook of where you have planted
each type and attach the seed packet to it.
That way you can always look at the packet if
you wish to read through any of the instructions.

Among the vegetables that you can grow are:
Lettuce—smaller varieties like Tom Thumb
and Little Gem are among the most successful. Make small sowings some weeks apart
and that will mean that the plants mature at

different times. For crisp and tender lettuce grow the plants on quickly with lots of water in a rich soil and harvest the plants when they are still young.

Radishes—these will really grow quickly for you. About a month after planting you can have lovely little plants that are ready for a salad or a sandwich. If you are adventurous you could even try for one of the new types which are yellow! Grow them where you have planted seed. Thinning may not be necessary but try to give them an inch apart so that they can develop.

Carrots—seeds will germinate in about three weeks but plants will take about 12 weeks before they are ready for harvesting. They need a good deep soil; are not happy in recently manured land. If you have heavy ground grow stumpy types. When you are thinning them do it very carefully. If you crush little plants the smell will reach carrot fly somewhere in the area and it can cause a lot of trouble.

Spring onions—these will be thinned out as they grow bigger and the little ones are quite appetising. Seed should germinate in three weeks but may be a little slow to move after that. Look out for White Lisbon which is the most popular of the salad varieties.

Herbs—many types can be grown success-fully. Beware of mint because it spreads its roots all over the place. Parsley can be hard to start … the seeds take ages to germinate but you could leave them in warm water overnight before planting them for a better chance of success. Try your hand with basil (you will find it used a lot in Italian dishes), chives (lovely when chopped with potatoes), marjo-ram (you will get its distinctive taste from chicken stuffing), rosemary (you will only need a little as it is very strongly flavoured). Be adventurous and you can have a wonderful herb garden. Just remember though that these do need a nice sunny spot for success.

Tomatoes—there are some grand little bush tomatoes that will grow quite happily out of doors as long as the soil is rich. They may need extra nitrogen but they will produce a lovely crop as the summer warms up. The seeds are easy to grow and like so many can be started on a windowsill where they will germinate within two weeks. You may need to put some straw under the bushes as they grow because fruit is often carried at ground level Look for varieties like Tiny Tim (you can grow this one in a window box!), Florida Petit (even smaller than Tiny Tim!), Pixie (although small may need staking) and Red Alert (a fairly new one that produces lots of fruit).

Potatoes—these will always seem too much of a problem but they can actually be grown in pots to give you your own very early potatoes. Get a couple of seed potatoes, talk nicely to your local seedsman and he will be happy to let you have a small amount. Plant them in black plastic pots that have been filled with a manure rich soil. (When handling anything to do with manure or chemicals always wear gloves). Just make sure that they are kept frost free. You could produce new potatoes for Christmas dinner by getting a few seedling potatoes as the first earlies come into the shops. Plant them in a well dug, well manured corner of the garden or in the black plastic pots. In late September cover them with a large cloche and that should be good enough to keep the frost away. Your crop will not be heavy so you may need four or five stalks growing to produce enough new potatoes. But what a surprise it will be to everyone!

11
Cacti

at Tail, Old Man, Fish Hook, Sea urchin, Sil ver Torch, Snowball, Strawberry.

That's only a few of the strange plants that exist in the world of the cacti...and when you see the plants you will immediately realise how they have come to get such odd names.

The Rat's Tail Cactus, for instance is a much prettier plant that its name suggests but it gets the name from the slender green stems that hang over the pot like tails but covered with sharp green spines. And the Old Man Cactus tells you what it is really like...it grows about 30 cm (1 ft) tall and is covered by white hairs that can be as long as 5 ins.

Growing cacti can be great fun and collecting them has become a very popular hobby in recent years. It has been estimated that there are about 2,000 different types of cactus available in the world so if you begin collecting you can go on building up that collection for years.

Cacti come generally from semi-desert areas of America and the West Indies. And although you generally see them without their flowers many of them do bloom with such a brillance that it can be startling. Their sizes too range from tiny little pot plants to those that can reach 1.8 m (about 6 ft) in height-and which, of course, would hardly be suitable for a collection on your windowsill!

The plants have developed their own way of saving water in their natural desert habitat but even there they do have heavy rainfalls that help replenish this water supply. And when you grow them you will have to take these needs very much into consideration. Just because they like a dry sandy way of life does not mean that they can exist for long periods without any water or other attention.

Their needs are, however, few once their environment has been established. This environment should consist of a warm, fairly dry atmosphere (preferably on a south facing windowsill) and an occasional heavy watering (which should, if possible, be rain water).This watering is very important when they are flowering.

They do have their own resting period—from November to March—when the temperature generally drops naturally for them. Like all resting plants they need very little watering at this time

How do you get started with cacti? Well, it is best to buy a plant from a nursery although you can start them yourself from seed. However they are not the easiest plants to raise in this way and seeds can take two years—and sometimes longer, to germinate. You can also grow them from cuttings which are best taken in May.

A gritty type of soil is what they need to grow well and clay type pots are the best to use because these dry out much faster than the plastic types. But do make sure that whatever containers you use are clean—and are kept clean.

They do need some feeding as well as watering—the best way to do this is to put some soluble fertiliser (like a liquid tomato fertiliser) in with their water when they are flowering.

Other than this their needs are few indeed and the plants will stay happily in their pots

for about four years. After this they should be repotted when you will find that they have just about filled their previous pot-home with roots.

The warning that has to be issued with them is to watch the spines or prickles which can be very sharp and can cause nasty cuts if not handled with care. The Column Cactus (Cereus Peruvianus) which is often the showpiece of the collector's display will quickly reveal its thorny side if mishandled. The long stem (it can reach to 90 cm—3 ft) is covered with brown spines. Many, many other cacti will have even more damaging spines so beware!

But once you have learned to treat the spiny stemmed ones with respect then you will have great fun finding out the very unusual ones that exist.

Here is a brief line-up of some that can be ideal subjects:

Bold Man Cactus (Cephalocereus senilis) will never flower for you but its tall column-like growth is entirely covered in long white hair.

Rat's Tail Cactus (Aporocactus flagelli-formis) is one of the easiest to grow and carries long flowers in the spring. A spiny one too.

Hedgehog cactus (Echinocereus pectinatus). A column-like spiny plant that carries pink, scented flowers.

Fish Hook Cactus (Ferocactus latispinus) Doesn't flower and gets its name for the brown spines that are very hooked.

Bunny ears (Optuntia Microdasys). Yes it lives up to its name and you will grow it for the oval pads with golden bristles that rise from the pot like a rabbit from the ground. Does not flower.

Powder Puff Cactus (Mammillaria bocasana). Dense white hairs giving this the look of silver; white flowers and hooked spines.

Living stones

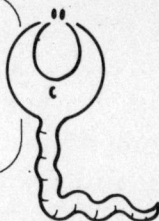

They are not cacti but they often form part of the cacti collection.

These are amazing plants as they mimic exactly the sort of stones that are found in their natural habitat. Their colours and patterns can be fascinating.There is a huge number of different plants available and they can easily be formed into a large collection.

The plant is formed by a pair of thick leaves that are fused together at the top and makes them look for all the world like stones. From between the leaves there usually appears a small daisy-like autumn flower.

They are very slow growing plants but after a few years the pot will be filled with clumps of stones that only show their tops over the soil but which underneath have a long tap root.

They are quite small in size from 13mm to 7 cm (1/2 - 2 ins.) and need to be kept absolutely dry in the winter.

Medicine plants

For many hundreds of years plants have been used as the basis for medicinal preparations—and they still are today. Go into any store or chemist's shop and search out the nature cures and you will find a huge number—such as garlic, hawthorn, mistletoe and hops being used as the main ingredient of many cures.

Plants have been taken way beyond the nature cure by scientists who have found that many ordinary garden plants have been helpful in fighting many diseases.

★ A plant called the Madagascar periwinkle has been found to provide wonderful help in the fight against children's leukemia and Hodgkin's Disease. This is a tropical plant but to make one single ounce of its wonderful extract 15 tons of the plant is needed in harvesting!

★ Closer to home the horse chesnut provides an extract for suntan creams.

★ The foxglove and the lily-of-the-valley provide a drug called digitalis that is used as a heart stimulant.

★ Poppies can provide a pain killing drug when their seeds are used.

★ The berbery hedge (*Berberis vulgaris*) can provide a medicine against fungal infections.

Many of these plants can however cause nasty illness — and some can even kill—if they are eaten raw. It is only their purified extract that is useful.

12

Danger— Some Plants Can Be Trouble!

Everyone avoids skin contact with nettles because they know they can sting—but there are many other plants that can be found in the garden that can also sting and poison too.

One of these is the lovely winter flowering Christmas Rose which is not a rose really but is one of the group of *Helleborus* plants—and stems and leaves of all plants in the group can cause skin irritation. The seeds, if eaten, will make you very ill. The herb Rue contains a poison which can also irritate the skin.

The *Euphorbia* is a plant that is often bought at Christmas time but also grows in the garden, The problem here is that the stems, when broke, drip a sticky white substance and this can cause eye infections.

So beware...don't eat parts of plants or berries unless you know that they are perfectly harmless. If you find that you have a rash coming out after handling a plant make sure that you get some medical attention immediately.

But don't panic. These things will only happen if you act carelessly or if you fail to take notice of any warnings that you have read about plants. Of course you can avoid a great deal of trouble if you constantly wear gloves or, if you have not been wearing them, you make sure that you scrub your hands clean when you have finished your task. Also try to avoid holding plants in your mouth, even if it is only for moment's convenience. Never rub your eyes with dirty hands or hands that have recently been handling plants.

If you want to avoid trouble in your garden take special care where the following plants are concerned. I am not placing them in special order other than putting the most commonly grown trouble makers at the top of the list. These are the most likely garden plants to cause you trouble but there are many other poisonous plants that grow wild.

Laburnum. Here is a beautiful shrub or tree that is also often called Golden Rain because of the long, drooping clusters of bright yellow summer flowers. The flowers are not troublesome but in the autumn when they have turned into long pods and produce seed they can be fatal if swallowed. The seed pods should be either picked off the tree before they set or gathered from the ground as they fall and disposed of safely.

Honeysuckle. It is one of nature's tragedies that this beautiful, heavily fragrant climber should also have to be listed among the troublesome plants. If the berries are eaten they will cause very painful tummy troubles.

Autumn Crocus. A simple little flower— but every part of it can be poisonous.

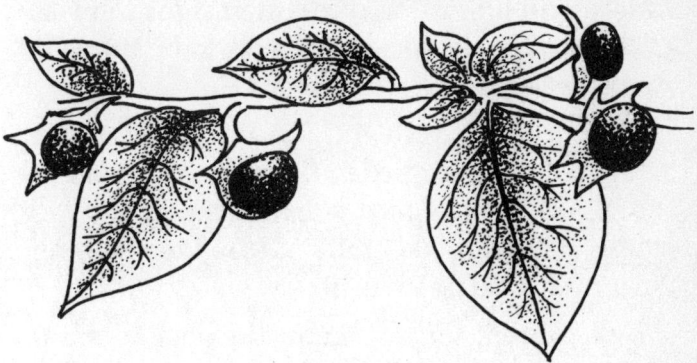

Foxglove. Another very popular garden flower but there is a poison in its rough and knotty leaves.

Mistletoe. Beware those lovely Christmas berries... they are highly poisonous and the plant, and any seasonal cuttings, should be treated with great care.

Lily of the Valley. Another wonderfully scented and lovely flower that hides its poison in the autumn berries.

Daphne (Daphne mezereum) Another of the sweet smelling plants that wait until autumn to produce poison in their red berries. This is a widely sold plant and a common sight in most gardens in early spring with its long. upright stems covered with red-purple flowers.

Columbine (aquilegia). It is one of those lovely old cottage garden flowers — but do not eat it! And in case that warning surprises you small children do put attractive looking flowers into their mouths.

Belladonna Lily (Amaryllis belladonna) This large trumpet like flower with a thick flower stalk may be hard to grow but many people do succeed. Its bulb is highly poisonous.

Arum Lily. The attractive red berries on this plant are the troublemakers.

Monkshood (Aconitum). A beautiful tall blue or violet flower that flaunts its poison in all parts of the plant with the tuberous root being fatal. The seeds and leaves can make a person very ill and because it carries its poison right through the plant it is regarded as the most dangerous of all plants in our gardens. Yet in science it can provide substances that are of great medicinal use.

Fool's parsley. If you have been brought up to eat parsley you might just pick some of the leaves from this one—but beware, it is a weed that is poisonous. You can distinguish it from real parsley by the fact that it carries small white flowers and the plant is much larger than edible parsley.

Euonymus. This is a tree that can be found in many shrubberies because of its good qualities. The berries are poisonous and so too are the leaves and bark.

Yew. These conifer type trees are often used for hedging as well as single specimen trees but both the leaves and the seeds are poisonous.

Nightshade. There are two types of this plant and while each is dangerous, the black berries of the Deadly Nightshade do live up to their name and can be fatal. The berries of the Woody Nightshade are also poisonous but not generally fatal unless eaten in large amounts —however they can cause violent illnesses.

Insect eating plants!

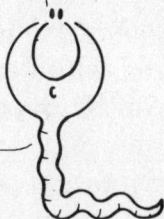

There are some plants that do a turnaround on nature—by living on insect and other animal life.

These are called carnivorous plants. Insects are often attracted by an unusual smell put out by the plant and then, when they land, they find that their way out of blocked by hairs or by the leaves closing on it. Sometimes they find themselves stuck in a special secretion put out by the plant. In most cases the plant gets its food from the liquid which comes from the insects as they decay.

Many of these plants can be found in damp, boggy places. One of these is the *Dorsea*, a small plant whose leaves sparkle in the sun but are covered with drops of sticky liquid. When an insect lands on the leaves it is trapped for the plant to eat!

And there is the very famous *Venus Fly-trap* the leaves of which stand open, but close immediately an insect lands on them.

There are many other plants of this type but they are not commonly grown in gardens. If however you would like to see some, visit the exotic plant house of your local Botanic Gardens.

13

Preserving Flowers

Flowers that are used for drying and preserving have a double advantage—they also give lots of colour in the garden during the summer. And they are easy to grow; just follow the instructions in Chapter two and you will find success.

But flowers that you grow for drying or preserving will last almost forever. The little heads often have to be wired because the stems will not do as long as the blooms but even this is simple nowadays with green wiring and tape that will give a very natural look.

The best way to use the flowers is for winter arrangements. All you need is a small square of Oasis (this is a foam-like material that comes in blocks and is available from most florists) and can be held in place with a pin holder. The pin holder is a very solid base with a number of pins and you just place the oasis on top of this. You may have to make holes in the Oasis for the stems but an easy way is to attach some wires to the base of the stems and they they can be easily moved about from place to place

Baskets make lovely containers for dried arrangements as they provide a simple shape but there is noting to stop you using anything including china, pottery, copper, brass or wood. Glass is not really acceptable because you can see the plant holder in the base. As well as that the weight of a pin holder can cause damage.

You will find that growing flowers for this hobby can be very rewarding because it will mean that you can make some pretty arrangements that will add colour to your room and home during the dull days of winter. And if the arrangement is put away with a light cover to keep dust off it can be brought out again the following winter to do its job again. All you need to do then is the brighten it up with a few more colourful flowers.

There are many flowers that preserve well — among the most popular are:

Straw Flower (Helichrysum). Look for one that is called *Helichrysum bracteatum* as this will give you the best flowers for drying. In one package of Helichrysum Dwarf Mixed you will get as many as 500 seeds for 50p! It will need a sunny, well drained spot and may need some staking to keep the stems straight. For drying it should be cut before the flowers are fully open. Hang them upside down in bunches in a dry, dust free spot in a garage or shed.

Bells of Ireland (Moluccella). This plant does not come from Ireland but from Syria. No doubt it got its name because of the green bell-like flowers. As it is not a very interesting flower it should be grown at the back of a border. Its main attraction is as a dried flower. For preserving cut the stem when the bells are fully open and dry them in a cool place away from direct sunlight.

Statice or Sea Lavender (Limonium). This is one of the most popular of all flowers for preserving and belongs to a group that are called 'everlasting flowers'. It prefers a nice light garden soil in a sunny spot. It comes in all colours although you will see it mostly as a papery-like purple in bunches for flower arrangers. One of the best is *Limonium suworowii* which has long, arching sprays of tiny pink flowers.

Acroclinium. This is an Australian flower which also goes under the name of *Helipterum* and is also often called the everlasting flower. Needs full sun and once planted the clumps should not be disturbed. A package usually of about 150 seeds will give you a wide range of colours in double and semi-double blooms.

Xeranthemum. This is a wild flower in parts of Europe but makes a very pretty garden flower too with flowers that are ideal for preserving. The blooms are daisy-like, strawy, crisp and hold their colour very well after drying. The flowers should be cut half open and dried by hanging upside down in a cool, airy place.

Chinese Lantern (Physalis). Here is a plant that you save for its seed pods rather the flowers. The seed pods do look very much like paper Chinese lanterns. It is a very adaptable plant and will grow anywhere in the garden and will do best in full or partial sun. Beware of one problem with this one—its roots grow and grow so it is best to keep it separate from the rest of the garden. However you can keep it as a tidy grower by trimming back the

clump of roots each year. For preserving cut
the stems in September and tie in small
bunches in a cool airy, place.

Honesty (Lunaria). It is a pretty but not very
noticeable flower in the summer garden. Its
chief benefit it for arranging in everlasting
arrangements. It isn't grown for the flowers
but for the attractive seed heads. These seed
heads are silvery white to greyish-green discs.
As soon as the seed pods begin to set the stems
should be cut.

Love-lies-bleeding (Amaranthus). This is a
plant with long tassels of either bright red or
pale green They need full sun as they are

basically tropical plants and they also need a lot of water in dry weather. The colours may fade somewhat after drying but they are still a very attractive plant. Just make sure when you are hanging them upside down to dry that the tassels do not get tangled.

Ornamental grasses. These are very important for those who want to use the dried flowers for arranging but they are not grown in the normal garden. You can buy packets of seeds but they should be planted in a spot away from the regular flowers. A search however in the countryside will often produce lots of grasses that are ideal for drying. Look too for some heads of barley, oats or wheat which are first class.

Pampas Grass (Cortaderia) If you really want something spectacular buy a small plant of pampas grass which will provide those great creamy plumes of bloom all summer long. The smallest version is *Cortaderia pumila*. These can cut and tear so make sure that you wear gloves when working with them. They dry well by hinging them upside down.

Ferns and bracken. There is a wealth of these available all over the place and you hardly need to grow them in your own garden at all. You should cut these as they are just beginning to lose colour and before they start to shrivel. Place them between newspapers and leave them under a weight for a few weeks. A good place to put the papers is under a carpet where they will not be disturbed and can dry out effectively.

Preserving the material
There are many sophisticated ways of preserving flowers and leaves but the most popular and easiest one to begin with is by drying.

The important thing is to make sure that you get the flowers just when they are at their right stage which is normally at almost their full beauty and just before they reach maturity. If you cut them too young they will shrivel and die and if you leave it too late they may disintegrate.

Cut a few flowers at a time. Trim away all the foliage and begin to work right away.

If you see some pretty petals beginning to fall off they can be held in place by a drop of clear nail varnish or clear glue. A small brush will be useful for the nail varnish and a toothpick will transfer the glue. Place them at the base of the petals where they meet the stems.

Should stems become brittle these can be wired. This will also keep them straight during drying.

Tie the flowers carefully into small bunches and place them in a cool, airy place. But try to keep them away from getting too dusty. A cupboard near a boiler room is ideal.

Flower heads should hang downwards as this will encourage the stems to stay straight. If you have a cupboard you can easily hang them from wire coat hangers, otherwise you can stretch them like washing on a line.

If you want to preserve leaves or ferns you can put them between newspapers and then, if possible under a carpet where they will not be disturbed. You can also iron them by placing them between waxed sheets of paper and coating the whole lot with sheets of newspaper. Set the iron above the minimum mark and just below the heat for synthetic fabrics. This is an operation where it is best to get some adult help as handling an iron on the paper can be dangerous.

Pot pourri

Pot pourri is that lovely mixture of dried flowers and spices kept in a jar and used to scent the air. It is simple to make and is a lovely gift when wrapped in pretty muslin or placed in a jar.

Rose petals are frequently the main ingredient although many, many types of scented flowers or even the secnted foliage of geraniums can be used.

Collect about a quart of unbruised rose petals after dew has dried on them but before the blooms lose their fragrance. Separate the petals and spread them out on a cloth to dry in the shade for 3-4 days.

Then mix together as many of the following spices and fragrances as you can find: A tablespoon each of powdered cloves, allspice, powdered orris root, ginger, nutmeg and about 2 tablespoons of cinnamon. If you can find some dried leaves of lemon verbena add them too. And if possible some drops of oil of jasmine.

When the rose petals are fully dried pack them into in layers, sprinkling each layer very lightly with some salt. First a layer of petals, then the salt, then a covering of the spices. When the jar is full allow to stand for about three weeks. Mix the collection together by shaking well and then distribute the pot pourri into various holders.

Cutting

There is really nothing quite as exciting as being able to cut a bunch of flowers from your own garden to take indoors or to give as a gift to a neighbour or friend. That is why if you are planting outside you should always give consideration to the types of plants—not all will give good cutting blooms. But having said that there are thousands that give exceptional cutting from January to December, or from daffodils to chrysanthemum.

You are actually doing your garden a favour by cutting blooms. Most plants will keep on flowering much longer if you remove the flowers either for decoration or when they have faded.

Flowers when cut should be placed in water immediately.The best time to do the cutting is early morning or late evening. Give them some hours in deep water before you arrange them. It is a good idea to cut flowers with a thick or woody stem under the water. Make the cut at an angle so that the stems will not sit flat on the bottom of the vase.

If flowers begin to wilt they can often be brought back to life by placing them in warm water for a few minutes.

14
Encouraging Wild Life in Your Garden

he birds and the bees and the butterflies will all find their way at some time to your garden but whether they stay or not depends on the welcome you give them.

There is much more wild life that you can encourage too...wild life like frogs and hedgehogs that will not cause damage to plants.

There is a great deal that anyone with even the smallest garden can do to encourage wild life to stay.

The first thing to do is to remember that many birds, butterflies and insects are attracted to the old-fashioned, sweet smelling plants. They also love areas where they can pop around in tall long grasses and hedges. So too do hedgehogs that live on slugs, beetles and worms and ignore the flowers and plants. Nettles and prickly plants like roses don't bother them either.

So your first task will be to create an area, an environment, where birds and animals will be happy and safe to live.

Birds
Begin by selecting the plants that will obviously attract the birds. These will be berried or hip-producing plants that they can eat. They will come searching for food, then they will look around for water, and finally for shelter. If you can provided this sort of area in your garden then birds will be very happy to nest there.

To make their nests they will need some thick hedges, shrub borders or trees and, of

course, evergreens are best. But whatever type of hedge grows in your garden it should be left untouched for a time so that the birds can happily set up nests there.

Begin to encourage birds by feeding them. This is an art in itself. You will often see the larger birds like pigeons, crows and magpies taking over a feeding spot and leaving the smaller birds to peck around outside the food area.

The best way to change this is to leave food on the ground for the larger birds but to provide a bird table for the others. This will have the added advantage of keeping the birds safe from family cats. Put a low roof on it and only the smaller birds can get inside to peck. You can put many sorts of scraps out including crusts, nuts, apple cores and such like. Hang string bags of nuts to the underside of the bird table and you will find that the smaller tits will land there and feed happily. Birds need some feeding all the year round but especially in the cold of winter and into spring when they are raising their young.

Birds also love the berries of hawthorn, holly, cotoneaster and pyracantha and many hedges so check up on any new plants that they have some sort of useful food for birds.

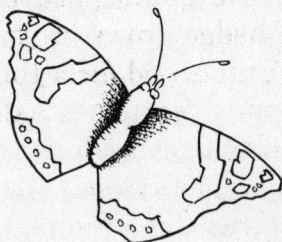

Birds also need water. If you have a pool, place a small board about an inch under the water and it will be very useful. In cold or freezing weather place out some water in a large flat container (the lid of a bin is very useful for this) and change it frequently.

Different birds have different approaches to nesting—some will make their homes in hedges, others in holes in old trees, others will appreciate a nesting box which should be placed out of the way of cats. Have only a small entrance to stop marauders and set it in a shady place; otherwise when spring comes around the baby birds could find themselves in a place where they could die from the heat.

Butterflies
Pity the poor butterfly. It is hated in its

juvenile form of caterpillar as it eats its way
through the gardener's favourite flowers and
vegetables but is always admired when it
emerges, often for a very brief few days of life
as a colourful butterfly. Some butterflies
however do live longer and need places in your
garden where they can hibernate safely away
from insecticides.

Butterflies love nettles... and indeed the
much hated stinging nettles are vital if you
wish to attract them to your garden. There is a
plant called Butterfly plant (horticulturally
the *Buddleia*) that they love and the range of
colours in this plant alone makes it an ideal
garden subject. Cornflowers, poppies
honeysuckle, lavender and many other sweet
smelling herbs and flowers are all ideal plants
to attract the butterfly, which, like most
insects, is able to locate plants by their
fragrances. They then drink the nectar from
the flowers.

Remember that the butterflies need a
warm, undisturbed corner in the garden
where their eggs will hatch out.

Hedgehogs
More and more these days many animals that
normally live in the wild have to search for

their homes in gardens. You will find squirrels, field and harvest mice and often find bats flying around at night. Frequently foxes turn towards domesticated gardens to search for prey. But the most domesticated of all the wandering animals seems to be the hedgehog.

Hedgehogs will exist in your garden quite independently of you or anyone else for that matter.

They hunt at night for a diet that is made up of slugs, snails, worms and insects, so there is nothing you can do to make their diet any different.

They sometimes do wander about by day but this is generally in midsummer when they play their courting games. They produce litters of small hedgehogs and they will often

make their nests at the base of a hedge.

They are simple little creatures, going about their business doing no one any harm.

Frogs

Long before I ever had a pond in my garden there were frogs about. They seemed to find lots of hiding places in a particularly damp patch behind my greenhouse and I had to go very carefully when it was tidying-up time in the autumn.

These particular frogs seem to have come from my neighbour's ponds where they had been encouraged to live by the placing of some frog's spawn around the water's edge.

You can buy frog's spawn and if you wish you can keep the spawn in a jar of pond water with some weed until the little black jelly-like spots begin to develop into tadpoles. It is fascinating to watch this development and you can actually see the first formation of life there in the jar.

But as the first legs begin to appear then it is time to move the little frogs out to their natural habitat. If you don't do this soon enough they will die as the weeds will not provide the necessary food. If you do wish to continue to keep a frog for a little while longer,

scraps of raw meat placed in the water will give it the necessary sustenance until it can get out to the pond and live there on the insects.

In a pool in your garden you can watch many more wonders of nature. And if you want to bring nature to your pool go to a local pond or stream and take back a jam jar full of sludge and put in the pond. In a few days this will have released a number of small insects and beetles that will be beneficial to a wild pond environment.

Using chemicals in your garden

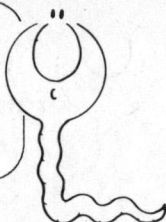

The reason that so many wonderful creatures are disappearing from our world is that they have been practically wiped out by sprays that are poisonous.

Chemicals that are made to kill weeds and harmful insects can also kill other wildlife. And it should be remembered that in destroying weeds they are also killing some beautiful wild plants…after all as someone has said a weed is just a plant whose beauty has not been discovered. Poet Gerald Manley Hopkins made his cry for wild gardens:

What would the world be, once bereft
Of wet and of wildness?
Let them be left,
O let them be left, wildness and wet;
Long love the weeds and the wilderness yet.

Of course the disappearance of the wilderness and weeds cannot be just put down to the use of chemicals in the fields of the world but they do play their part. Most manufactures however go out of their way to tell you which creatures will not be harmed by their sprays but they do tell you the ones that can affected.

Before anyone uses a spray of any kind in the garden the instructions should be read very carefully. If they say it is dangerous they mean it. If you should be about when anyone is spraying you should wear overall clothing and even a face mask. I know it always seems like something from *Dr Who* or *Star Trek* but it could save you a lot of distress.

The best way for the true wildlife corner of your garden is to keep it free of any chemicals.

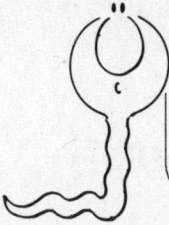

How to cope with garden pests without using chemicals

Here are some ideas that you may like to try should you have difficulties with aphides or other sucking creatures in the garden.

Lure aphids away from the plants by putting out a small tin which has been painted a bright yellow inside. Fill it with soapy water and the insects that are attracted by the bright colour will be drowned in the water.

If this bothers you then just make up a dip or spray of chopped red peppers, garlic and soapy water. The aphids won't stay to ask questions.

Tobacco extracts (buy a small bag of tobacco) watered into the ground will not harm the plant but will eliminate many root eating troublemakers.

Cockroaches which are harmful to plants can be eliminated by putting down a dust of boric acid.

Red spider mite which is becoming a worldwide nuisance will be wiped out with a spray made up of buttermilk, flour and soap! Leave it on the plants for a few hours and then hose the plant down.

Try these remedies and see!

15
Your Garden Diary

Spring

The ground is warming up and growth will begin very soon.

Get any designs finished as soon as possible. Make sure the ground is absolutely clear of weeds and old roots and any other rubbish that may have collected over winter.

If you have some miniature roses they can be pruned quite tightly, but do it early in spring so that new growth is moving along for early flowers.

Begin planting annual seeds, making sure that you mark exactly where you have placed the different types. Sow them thinly to avoid overcrowding and waste.

Half-hardy annuals and others can also be planted but they should be kept indoors until all chance of frost has passed.

Vegetables should be treated in most cases like the annual seeds so it is time now to begin to get lettuce and radish and others moving.

Many seeds will be through in a matter of weeks—so too will the first of the annual weeds. Keep the weeds down when they are small and that will stop them reseeding.

The early months of spring can often be very dry so make sure that all established plants are watered. Older plants will need a good watering but seedlings will only need water filtered on gently with a fine rose on the watering can.

As foliage on tulips and daffodils dies away clean it up. Daffodils should be left on in the ground but tulips should be dug and stored. If you have large clumps of snowdrops, lift and divide them while the foliage is still green.

Summer

This is the time to enjoy all the plants that you have been growing but you will also have to make sure that they can be kept on growing at their very best.

To keep them growing, water them regularly and add a little liquid feed to the water each time. With annuals and soft plants little and often is usually better then one great watering and feeding.

Finish planting out any seedlings that you have raised yourself.

If you have not sown enough seeds buy some boxes of plants and get them into the soil immediately. Only buy plants that look strong and healthy and contented. Water them in well.

Try to avoid moving plants at this time of the year but if you must, then make sure that they have as little root disturbance as possible. As soon as they have been replanted in either the soil or in a pot, water them very well.

In the vegetable garden you can plant out the runner beans and make successive sowings of lettuce and radish so that they won't all grow at once. Tomatoes too can be planted out early in summer and if they are the bush types will not need any cover.

The greatest trouble in the garden will be from slugs...discourage them in any way you can!

Weeds must be kept down; otherwise they will strangle all the flowers and vegetables and undo all your good work.

Don't forget to collect the everlasting flowers and hang them up to dry.

Autumn

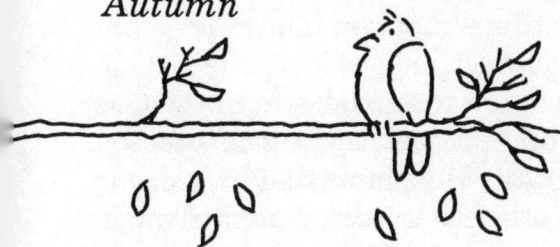

Americans call this the Fall—and it is a good name. It is the herald of falling leaves and dying flowers. But there are still a lot of wonderful things happening in the gardens...and work that can be done.

Flowers will deep on blooming for much longer if they are dead-headed. This means cutting off the blooms before they have fully died down and begun to set seeds. If you wish to harvest some seed from plants then allow flowers to stay on until they have formed their own seed pod which should be cut off when it is starting to dry out. Store the seeds in a cool, dark place until the spring when they can be sown.

The first frosts will cause many plants to die down. To keep the garden looking tidy just dig up the dead plants and use them for compost. If, however, there are tubers or bulbs these should be taken up and saved for planting the next time around.

This is the time to plant for next year. Decide what part of the garden you are going to use for your very own and begin to clean it up. New soil dug up now can be left loose so that winter frosts will help break it down.

Also clean pots and containers so that when you get some seed (much can be planted now) everything is at the ready.

Winter

There will not be much that you can do in the garden now...but there is a lot that you can plan for the next year.

If you draw up your plans now it will mean that you can get orders in for seed. Send away for a catalogue (you will find them advertised in the gardening papers); not only will it give you the names of flowers but many of them contain lots of useful information too.

If you have been growing plants that may be regarded as tender (like geraniums) make sure that they are well housed out of the way of frosts.

Bulbs can still be planted...but November is about the last chance you will get of planting daffodil and tulip bulbs so that they will produce their best flowers in the spring.

It is the right time to plant roses as it allows the roots to get settled in their new home before the spring growing push begins.

Mistletoe

Everyone would like to have a spray of mistletoe at Christmas and wouldn't it be wonderful to be able to cut some from your own garden?

But it has a sort of magic about it and few gardeners want to grow it—and the reason? Probably because it is a parasite...in other words it needs a host tree on which to live, something like the cuckoo taking another bird's nest.

The tree that it seems to like best is the apple but it has been known to grow on poplar, hawthorn, maple and even on oak trees.

You will have to impregnate a tree after Christmas by using a berry from a spray that you have purchased or received from somewhere else.

Pick the mistletoe berry and squash it into cracks or crevices in the bark of a suitable tree. Select the sunless side of the tree as this will give the seeds the greatest chance of germinating and growing.

You will have to make a number of impregnations to make sure that it will take—and it will be some time before you know if you are successful. But think of the fun when you can cut your own branch for Christmas.

Do however be careful—the pods are poisonous so do not swallow any and make sure that you wash your hands carefully after you have crushed them.